IN PLACE OF FEAR

Aneurin Bevan

Aneurin Bevan

In Place of Fear

★

With a Foreword by
JENNIE LEE

Republished by
EP Publishing Limited
1976

First published 1952. This edition reprinted from the
1961 edition, published by MacGibbon & Kee Ltd.,
London

Republished 1976 by
EP Publishing Limited
East Ardsley, Wakefield
West Yorkshire, England

ISBN 0 7158 1168 1

Please address all enquiries to EP Publishing Limited
(address as above)

Printed in Great Britain by
The Scolar Press Limited
Ilkley, West Yorkshire

TO JENNIE

Contents

Illustrations

A*

Foreword
To the 1976 edition

By JENNIE LEE

ANEURIN BEVAN regarded *In Place of Fear* as a series of shorthand notes on themes he planned to write about at greater length later on. Even as such there is too much of his essential self in this book for it to be allowed to go out of print. It remains urgently contemporary. Indeed we have a long way to go before we catch up.

Nye regarded imaginative tolerance as the mark of a civilised mind. He himself had it to an extraordinary degree. However alien the company, no matter how many barriers of race, religion, language, age, and social customs stood between, he could, when he chose, vault over the lot as if they did not exist, and be right there at the heart of their lives and problems. In gaols, slums, palaces, cathedrals, in vast public assemblies, in the strict privacy of a gathering of intimate friends, I have seen this happen again and again.

It was not a trick. It was simply that he had a seemingly inexhaustible capacity for living, for loving, for seeing the fun and absurdity of life as well as its tragic side. In the last chapter of this book he writes: "Not even the apparently enlightened principle of 'the greatest good for the greatest number' can excuse indifference to individual suffering. There is no test for progress other than its impact on the individual. If the policies of statesmen, the enactments of legislatures, the impulses of group activity, do not have for their object the enlargement and cultivation of the individual life, they do not deserve to be called civilised."

That was Nye. The brusque tongue, the astringent judgment, deceived no-one who was close to him. Private living he adored. Public chores he detested. But a fierce tenderness and an inescapable involvement in all the great issues of our times impelled him onwards into one hard fight after another.

I cannot remember a time in all the years we were together when he was not fighting against impossible odds. I can hear him bounding up the stairs, two or three steps at a time, to the top flat where we lived during the first two years of our married life. The door would be thrown open, he would come hurrying in, spilling over with news and excitement. 'Here we go again. A wooden cross or a golden crown'. That was a kind of theme song. I knew it meant the beginning of a period of intense physical, emotional, intellectual

11

exertion, no holds barred, while he was fighting to rouse public opinion, particularly in the more lethargic sections of our own Labour movement, to the imminence of war, the crime of betraying Spain, the need for the Labour Party to adopt a less drearily conservative type of socialism.

Nye's socialism had the radiant, elegant quality of his own personality. He was as likely to express it in terms of José Rodo as of Karl Marx. His many-sidedness meant that he retained at all times what he himself would call 'the gift of the unexpected.' But this did not mean any vacillation of purpose. Again and again he gave this warning: "The chief enemy of democratic socialism is vacillation, for it must achieve passion in action in pursuit of qualified judgments. It must know how to enjoy the struggle, while recognising that progress is not the elimination of struggle but rather its change in terms. It must seek the truth in any given situation, knowing all the time that if this be pushed too far it falls into error."

I was sometimes astonished by the extent and diversity of the lines of communication Nye somehow maintained with rebel movements all over the world. Official contacts with heads of government and leading members of Opposition parties is one thing. But how was it that in remote parts of Africa, Asia, South America, and elsewhere, unknown men and women, making their first tentative efforts against oppression, somehow knew he was there, their comrade, with them in spirit, and on the alert to lend a practical helping hand to the limit of his resources. I don't quite know. But somehow they knew. Maybe it was partly because he was incapable of the illiteracy of reducing the complexities of the modern world to crude black and white terms. 'This is my truth; now tell me yours' was one of his favourite quotations.

"What is the use" he insisted, "of taunting the under-developed countries with the absence of democratic institutions if these can survive only by a slower rate of economic progress or by help from outside? When we were at their economic level we were hanging children and driving them into the mines and into the mills, and organising labour camps in the countryside."

There is no hint of patronage in that kind of language, nor again when he asks us to keep in mind that "Mankind is not born with an insatiable appetite for political liberty. This is the coping-stone on the structure of progress, not its base. If political liberty and the institutions that enshrine it were spontaneous imperatives of the human spirit, our task would be much easier. But they are earth-bound and time-bound. The pulse of progress beats differently for different parts of the world, and if we are to understand what is happening around us and act intelligently about it, we must recognise that fact and realise that once we stood where they now stand."

The written word is a poor substitute for the kind of bond Nye so often established between himself and his immediate audience. But it has one supreme advantage. He is still putting his own point of view. There is no need for anyone, deliberately or otherwise, to falsify his values.

Aneurin Bevan was a passionate parliamentarian. The years of mass unemployment between the two world wars taught him the limits of direct industrial action. Indeed, the lesson was graphically underlined by David Lloyd George as early as 1919, when he told the leaders of the Triple Alliance of that time: "Gentlemen, if you call out the miners, the transport workers and the railwaymen, you have us at your mercy. But if a force arises in the State stronger than the State itself it must be prepared to take on the functions of the State. Have you considered these consequences and are you ready?"

The trade union movement was most certainly not ready; nor again when it called a General Strike in 1926. There was no short cut to power. A parliamentary majority had to be won, and once that happened a Labour government had to prove itself capable of governing. The one situation, Nye insisted, that was fatal for a democratic parliament was helplessness in face of economic difficulties.

Here you have the key to the recurrent and often bitter conflicts between Aneurin Bevan and the defenders of official Labour Party policy. He was at all times vividly conscious that Parliamentary institutions like all else are 'earth-bound and time-bound'. We had to reach a certain stage of economic development before we could enjoy the privilege of a parliament elected by universal franchise. It was illiterate and cruel to taunt countries that had not reached this point with the fact that they lacked our liberties. But most important of all, it was a betrayal of the job we had to do if, having won a parliamentary majority, we did not demonstrate that parliament was 'a weapon, the most formidable weapon of all, in the struggle to redress economic wrongs'.

How was this to be done? Certainly not by leaving parliament with responsibility, and private property with power. 'If economic power' Nye insisted, 'is left in private hands, and a distressed people ask parliament in vain for help, its authority is undermined. Its role is reduced to that of a public mourner for private economic crimes'.

A lifelong duel was fought between Conservative traditionalists and this socialist concept of the new functions of parliament in the mid-twentieth century. We are still in the midst of the argument. It has not yet been settled one way or another. Nor does it help if we make long-term judgments based on the circumstances of the passing moment. Unless socialists are prepared to forego the lazy luxury of living from hand to mouth all the hopes, all the dedicated service, all the hard serious thought that has brought us to our present strength will turn to nothing. Indeed that is an understatement. The process of undermining the authority of the elected chamber has already gone dangerously far. It is being filtered off to the House of Lords, to a narrow group of press lords and business executives, to the other side of the Atlantic and the Channel.

There was a short period of time following 1945 when the eyes of the world turned towards Westminster, half-wondering, half-unbelieving. A Conservative opposition was fighting with formidable intensity to prevent a Labour Government healing war wounds and rebuilding the economy on a sounder and juster foundation. Our prestige throughout the world was high then. It is now embarrassingly low. For reasons that lie in history, not in the personal virtues or vices of its opponents, Conservative Governments are deaf and blind to the contemporary spirit. Individual conservatives, even in the leadership ranks, sometimes try to break through. But they cannot have it both ways. They cannot draw their sustenance, materially and otherwise, from ancient vested interests, and at the same time not expect to be brought to heel by those interests.

Conscious of this, Nye fought to the limits of his strength and beyond for the socialist values that he believed to be 'the only ones broadly applicable to the situation in which mankind now finds himself.' *In Place of Fear* was first published in 1952. Since then there has been a considerable improvement in the standard of life of most working people. But the hardest test has still to come. Much that has been gained can be lost. We can lose confidence in political democracy. We can turn instead to direct confrontation. We can set forces in motion that lead inexorably to civil war.

Aneurin Bevan never indulged in facile optimism. Always he said "there is a question mark over our future". Would we have vision and resilience enough to understand in time that "Each freedom is made safe only by adding another to it. Democracy is protected by extending its boundaries. The emergence of modern industry, with its danger of depersonalisation of the worker, challenges the vitality of democratic principles. In the societies of the West, industrial democracy is the conterpart of political freedom, Liberty and responsibility march together in the workshop as in the legislative assembly. Only when this is accomplished shall we have the foundations of a buoyant and stable civilisation."

When first written a quarter of a century ago such reflections were dismissed as mere idealistic theorising. Now, whether or not we can create more all-embracing forms of democratic participation has become an urgent item on the agenda of every political and industrial conference. Indeed, many leading industrialists as well as trade union leaders have come to accept that our best hope of economic advance—maybe our only hope—lies in this direction.

I have not attempted in any way to alter the original text. Such statistics, therefore, as are used by way of illustration relate to social and economic conditions a quarter of a century ago. As such, they are not without interest to the student of history. But it is the essential philosophy set out in the following chapters with its relevance to present-day problems, that makes this new edition worth while.

Not even the apparently enlightened principle of the 'greatest good for the greatest number' can excuse indifference to individual suffering . . .

ANEURIN BEVAN

IN PLACE OF FEAR

1

Poverty, Property and Democracy

In many ways it would have been better for a book of this sort to have been written by a person detached from day-to-day preoccupation with political affairs. Yet, as I come to write, I begin to see that there are advantages possessed by a political practitioner like myself that are denied to anyone living a more cloistered life; for in the pattern of my own activities have been woven the main strands of the political epoch which began with the end of the great war of 1914–1918.

I started my political life with no clearly formed personal ambition as to what I wanted to be, or where I wanted to go. I leave that nonsense to the writers of romantic biographies. A young miner in a South Wales colliery, my concern was with the one practical question: Where does power lie in this particular state of Great Britain, and how can it be attained by the workers? No doubt this _man of_ is the same question as the one to which the savants of political _learning_ theory are fond of addressing themselves, but there is a world of difference in the way it shaped itself for young workers like myself. It was no abstract question for us. The circumstances of our lives made it a burning, luminous mark of interrogation. Where was power and which the road to it?

It will be seen at once that the question formulated itself in different fashion for us than it would have done in a new, pioneering society or in the mind of someone equipped by a long formal education. In such cases the question shapes itself in some such fashion as, 'How can I get on?' or, 'What career shall I choose?' I don't mean by this that we were necessarily less selfish. It was merely that the texture of our lives shaped the question into a class and not into an individual form. We were surrounded by the established facts of the Industrial Revolution. We worked in pits, steelworks,

21

foundries, textiles, mills, factories. These were the obvious instruments of power and wealth. The question therefore did not form
itself for us in some such fashion as, 'How can I buy myself a steelworks, or even a part of one?' Such possibilities were too remote to
have any practical import.) *meaning, importance.*

Then again, we had a long tradition of class action behind us
stretching back to the Chartists. So for us power meant the use of
collective action designed to transform society and so lift all of us
together. To us the doctrine of *laissez-faire* conveyed no inspiration, because the hope of individual emancipation was crushed by
the weight of accomplished power. We were the products of an
industrial civilization and our psychology corresponded to that fact.
Individual ambition was overlaid by the social imperative. The
streams of individual initiative therefore flowed along collective
channels already formed for us by our environment. Society
presented itself to us as an arena of conflicting social forces and not
as a plexus of individual striving.

These forces are in the main three: private property, poverty and
democracy. They are forces in the strict sense of the term, for they
are active and positive. Among them no rest is possible.

I imply here no narrow definition of poverty, although heaven
knows there is enough of that. I mean the general consciousness of
unnecessary deprivation, which is the normal state of millions of
people in modern industrial society, accompanied by a deep sense
of frustration and dissatisfaction with the existing state of social
affairs. It is no answer to say that things are better than they were.
People live in the present, not in the past. Discontent arises from a
knowledge of the possible, as contrasted with the actual. There is a
universal and justifiable conviction that the lot of the ordinary man
and woman is much worse than it need be. That is all I need to have
admitted for my present purposes.

This discontent must be aimed at something, and naturally it is
aimed at wealth and at those who, by possession of wealth, have a
dominating influence on the policy of the nation. And third, there
is the political democracy which put a new power in the possession
of ordinary men and women.

The conflict between the forces, always implicit, breaks out into open struggle during periods of exceptional difficulty, like widespread and prolonged unemployment, and exposes the government of the day and the political constitution to great strain. Sometimes, as in Germany, the constitution breaks under it. It was not the Treaty of Versailles that broke the Weimar Constitution of Germany. It was unemployment. Hitler talked in vain when the German was in work. Loss of work is also loss of status. When Hitler raved about the low status of Germany among the nations, it was a dramatic representation of the lack of status of every unemployed worker who listened to him. It is not necessary to believe in the 'economic man' to accept this.

The fact is that the Germans had already started to turn away from him as unemployment began to decline. A little later and he would have failed. The Weimar Republic had survived the Versailles Treaty. It could not survive both the Versailles Treaty and unemployment for six or seven million Germans. The decisive factor was the unemployment.[1]

The issue therefore in a capitalist democracy resolves itself into this: either poverty will use democracy to win the struggle against property, or property, in fear of poverty, will destroy democracy. Of course, the issue never appears in such simple terms. Different flags will be waved in the battle in different countries and at different times. And it may not be catastrophic unemployment. There may be a slower attrition as there was in Britain before the war, but poverty, great wealth and democracy are ultimately incompatible elements in any society.

This is the answer to so many people who see freedom in a vacuum. A free people will always refuse to put up with preventable poverty. If freedom is to be saved and enlarged, poverty must be ended. There is no other solution. The problem of how to prevent these three forces from coming into head-on collision is the principal study of the more politically conscious Conservative leaders. How can wealth persuade poverty to use its political freedom to keep wealth in power? Here lies the whole art of Conservative politics in the twentieth century.

In so far as politics is a struggle between competing ideas and ideals, these accrete around one or other of the three forces. As a

growth , something
added on.

general rule the combatants are aware only of the ideas and ideals which actuate them, and this fact enables them to generate passion and to become capable often of ennobling self-sacrifice and altruism. But all the time these qualities are mobilized in the service of the dynamic thrust arising from the interplay of the dominating forces working around and through them.

To contend that this is a cynical view of the part played by individuals in politics is to deny the possibility of a systematic study of the behaviour of groups of individuals acting together in society. When we make such generalizations about past behaviour it is called social.science. Why should it be called cynicism or mechanistic determinism when the same method is used to explain what is happening around us at the moment? Or does it mean that the essence of idealism is to be ignorant of why we do what we do, when we do it?

I am not asserting that when social reformers are moved to ease the distress of poor people they are thinking of the minimum concession necessary to preserve the rule of wealth. What I do contend is that the suffering of the poor was ignored while they lacked the power and status to insist on alleviation.

One experience remains vividly in my memory. While the miners were striking in 1926 a great many people were moved to listen to their case. Certain high ecclesiastical dignitaries even went so far as to offer to mediate between the mine owners and the miners. They were convinced that the terms the coal owners were attempting to impose upon the miners were unreasonable and would entail much suffering and poverty for hundreds of thousands of miners' homes. Their efforts failed. The miners were beaten and driven back to work under disgraceful conditions.

For years these conditions continued. But were those high Church dignitaries moved to intervene then? Not at all. For them the problem was solved. It had never consisted in the suffering of the miners, but in the fact that the miners were still able to struggle and therefore create a problem for the rest of the community. The problem was not their suffering but their struggle. Silent pain evokes no response. The social reforms of the twentieth century are a consequence of the democratic power of the masses and not of increased enlightenment. Enlightenment has grown with the emergence of political freedom and it will diminish if freedom declines.

Political democracy brings the welfare of ordinary men and women on to the agenda of political discussion and demands its consideration.

Fascism and all forms of authoritarian government take it off the agenda again.

The political high priests of wealth-privilege are acutely conscious of the unbridgeable antagonism between private wealth, poverty and political democracy. They are never statesmen conceiving it to be their duty to advance society beyond the poverty age. Their job as they see it is to beguile democracy into voting wealth back into power at each election. For this they adapt their language and shape their plans. When the people are behaving as they wish them to behave, they say complacently: 'The British people are sound at heart.' When the people look like turning them down they begin to see the 'defects of democracy as a permanent system of government', and warn us that 'we must distinguish between freedom and licence'. When we do as they want us to do, it is freedom. When we suit ourselves, it is licence.

The function of parliamentary democracy, under universal franchise, historically considered, is to expose wealth-privilege to the attack of the people. It is a sword pointed at the heart of property-power. The arena where the issues are joined is Parliament.

The atmosphere of Parliament, its physical arrangements, its procedure, its semi-ecclesiastical ritual, are therefore worth careful study. They are all profoundly intimidating for the products of a board school system who are the bearers of a fiery message from the great industrial constituencies. The first essential in the pioneers of a new social order is a big bump of irreverence.

'The past lies like an Alp upon the human mind.' The House of Commons is a whole range of mountains. If the new Member gets there too late in life he is already trailing a pretty considerable past of his own, making him heavy-footed and cautious. When to this is added the visible penumbra of six centuries of receding legislators, he feels weighted to the ground. Often he never gets to his feet again.

His first impression is that he is in church. The vaulted roofs and stained-glass windows, the rows of statues of great statesmen of the past, the echoing halls, the soft-footed attendants and the whispered conversation, contrast depressingly with the crowded meetings and the clang and clash of hot opinions he has just left behind in his election campaign. Here he is, a tribune of the people, coming to make his voice heard in the seats of power. Instead, it seems he is expected to worship; and the most conservative of all religions – ancestor worship.

The first thing he should bear in mind is that these were not his ancestors. His forebears had no part in the past, the accumulated dust of which now muffles his own footfalls. His forefathers were tending sheep or ploughing the land, or serving the statesmen whose names he sees written on the walls around him, or whose portraits look down upon him in the long corridors. It is not the past of his people that extends in colourful pageantry before his eyes. They were shut out from all this; were forbidden to take part in the dramatic scenes depicted in these frescoes. In him his people are there for the first time, and the history he will make will not be merely an episode in the story he is now reading. It must be wholly different; as different as is the social status which he now brings with him.[2]

To preserve the keen edge of his critical judgement he will find that he must adopt an attitude of scepticism amounting almost to cynicism, for parliamentary procedure neglects nothing which might soften the acerbities of his class feelings. In one sense the House of Commons is the most unrepresentative of representative assemblies. It is an elaborate conspiracy to prevent the real clash of opinion which exists outside from finding an appropriate echo within its walls. It is a social shock absorber placed between privilege and the pressure of popular discontent.

The new Member's first experience of this is when he learns that passionate feelings must never find expression in forthright speech. His first speech teaches him that. Having come straight from contact with his constituents, he is full of their grievances and his own resentment, and naturally, he does his best to shock his listeners into some realization of it.

He delivers himself therefore with great force and, he hopes and fears, with considerable provocativeness. When his opponent arises to reply he expects to hear an equally strong and uncompromising answer. His opponent does nothing of the sort. In strict conformity with parliamentary tradition, he congratulates the new Member upon a most successful maiden speech and expresses the urbane hope that the House will have frequent opportunities of hearing him in the future. The Members present endorse this quite insincere sentiment with murmurs of approval. With that, his opponent pays no more attention to him but goes on to deliver the speech he had intended to make. After remaining in his seat a little longer, the new Member crawls out of the House with feelings of deep relief at having got it over, mingled with a paralysing sense of frustration. The stone he thought he had thrown turned out to be a sponge.

I would not have bothered to describe this typical experience of a working man speaking in the House of Commons for the first time were it not characteristic of the whole atmosphere. The classic parliamentary style of speech is understatement. It is a style unsuited to the representative of working people because it slurs and mutes the deep antagonisms which exist in society.

It was not until the General Election of 1929 that a British parliament was elected on the basis of complete adult suffrage. The historical function of Liberalism was to achieve the sovereignty of the people in Parliament, and having done so, to seek to confine parliamentary activity to a miminum. The Liberal revolution found power concentrated in the hands of the great landlords, rising in hierarchical ascent to the Crown. As the ownership of property became dispersed, with the rise of urban development, a corresponding dispersal of political power seemed the obvious and natural course. Once that had been accomplished, Liberalism was emptied of its historical purpose.

Thomas Jefferson was keenly aware of this.* The franchise and all that went with it was the political articulation of private property held in comparatively small quantities. In its idealistic pronouncements Liberalism asserted the right of the people to be consulted in

*See S. K. Padover, *Jefferson*, New York: Harcourt, Brace, 1942; p. 297.

the making of national policy, but in its practical application it was the assertion of dispersed against concentrated property power. The history of the development of the franchise in Britain is conclusive proof of this. Once the Liberal Party had established itself in Parliament it was in no hurry to extend the franchise. Indeed, from that point onwards, the unenfranchised were merely a counter in the electoral battles between the Conservatives and the Liberals. This, along with the traditional tenacity of masculine values, explains why a Liberal government opposed the feminine franchise. Women as such were apparently not people.

It is necessary to distinguish between the intention of Liberalism and its achievement. Its intention was to win power for the new forms of property thrown up by the Industrial Revolution. Its achievement was to win political power for the people irrespective of property. In saying this I am not trying to detract from the genuine idealism of the best spokesmen of the Liberal era. They reached out for the complete realization of their ideals with the utmost sincerity, but with the accomplishment of their inherited historical task, the thrust of the energy which inspired them declined. Decades elapsed before their best perorations were realized.

Political democracy in Britain is only a little more than twenty-one years old. It is necessary to emphasize this, because so many people confuse the existence of Parliament with that of a democracy. Parliament in Britain is centuries old. Democracy has only just come of age. In 1929, when I was elected to Parliament for the first time, I was a member of the first British Parliament elected by all men and women over twenty-one years of age.

So much has been written about the failure of modern democracy to grapple successfully with the problems of the time that it is well to keep in mind this immaturity of democracy as a political institution. Incessant propaganda is aimed at making the people believe that they have held power for a long time and that the present state of affairs is the result of their failure to use it properly, when in fact they have hardly started to use it at all. In this fashion the people have their self-confidence undermined and the way is prepared to hand power over to a class of so-called exceptional people, or to a Leader who is assumed to have the virtues they are supposed to lack.

This subtle attack on the self-confidence of democracy has gone very far. It is responsible for many of the shortcomings of the Socialist experiments in Britain. One of the main functions of this book is to get the whole question into better perspective. For the moment, however, I am concerned with the impact of the arrival of the people's representatives at Westminster and with the atmosphere and physical organization of the House of Parliament.

The function of Parliament as an instrument of social change has received inadequate attention from students of political theory. With the completion of universal franchise the Liberal era ended. At this point Liberal and Conservative theories combine. Both assign a negative function to Parliament. With the destruction of the political power of the great landlords and the limitation of the powers of the Crown, along with the rise of urban property, the main function of Parliament was to raise whatever taxes were necessary to maintain the armed forces; and then to 'keep the ring'.

To this conception everything at Westminster is subservient. It dominates the actual physical arrangements of the Houses of Parliament, the procedure of the House of Commons, and the attitude to the Civil Service. That government is best which governs least is still the traditional and indeed the philosophical attitude of both the Liberal and the Conservative Parties. Where they have departed from it they have done so reluctantly, and even then usually only under the impact of war conditions and necessities.

So much is this the case that a distinguished civil servant told me in 1945, on the occasion of my taking office at the Ministry of Health, that he could not conceive even a start being made toward British national recovery with the machinery of government as it was before the war. The Labour government of 1945 inherited from the war a system of wartime controls and disciplines which could not have been realized in normal conditions without something approaching a revolution.

I have already referred to the effect of the atmosphere of Parliament on the new Labour Member. The physical facilities prepared for him are fantastic in their inadequacy. Some people focus attention on the smallness of the debating chamber. They point out that all the Members cannot find seats. This is really of little importance.

The size of the chamber is a compromise between accommodation and the kind of intimate debate in which the British Parliament excels. Speaking for myself, I prefer the existing size. A large chamber would encourage a style of speech more declamatory without necessarily being more forthright, and usually at odds with the kind of business Parliament has to discuss. The present chamber can house with felicity the intimate conversational style suitable to committee discussion, and at another time the grand theatre of a great public debate.

It is with the physical arrangements outside the chamber that I quarrel, for they are steeped in class bias. They are based on the assumption that Members of Parliament are well-to-do and possess houses within easy reach of the House of Commons. This is no longer the case to the extent of former times.

Now that the state has stepped in as a permanent instrument of intervention in economic affairs, it is necessary to revise the relationship between the private Member and the government, especially as regards the facilities placed at the disposal of the former. The new House of Commons has gone some way to meet the need, but more, much more, is needed if the vast state apparatus is to be brought and kept under effective democratic control. If the membership of the House of Commons is to be composed of men and women of moderate means, which is most desirable, who normally have their homes in their constituencies, then clerical and office facilities should be put at their disposal.[3]

It is nonsense to complain of an immense and tendentiously all-powerful Civil Service, and at the same time cavil at the small expenditure required to equip the elected representatives responsible for controlling its actions with the means to do so adequately.

These may seem to some to be matters of detail out of place in a work of this nature. After more than twenty-two years' membership of the House of Commons, I disagree. The effectiveness of democracy depends to a considerable extent on the facilities afforded its representatives. If they are crippled in their work their constituents suffer a corresponding curtailment of authority.

From 1929 onwards in Great Britain the stage was set and all the actors assembled in the great drama which is the essence of politics in modern advanced industrial communities. First, there was wealth, great wealth, concentrated in comparatively few hands, although cushioned by a considerably developed middle class. Second, there was a working class forming the vast majority of the nation and living under conditions which made it deeply conscious of inequality and preventable poverty. Third, there was fully developed political liberty, expressing itself through constitutional forms which had matured for many centuries and had as their central point an elected assembly commanding the respect of the community.

There were also political parties roughly corresponding with the class divisions, but with varying degrees of political self-consciousness. The situation anticipated and feared by Oliver Cromwell as long ago as 1647 had arrived.*

NOTE 1

The average annual unemployment figures in Germany from 1924 to 1933 were as follows:

1924	911,000
1925	646,000
1926	2,011,000
1927	1,353,000
1928	1,353,000
1929	1,692,000
1930	3,076,000
1931	4,520,000 } with a maximum of 6,500,000
1932	5,603,000 } in the winter 1931/32
1933	4,733,000

In the Elections of 31 July, 1932, Adolf Hitler obtained 13,732,779 votes. A little over three months later (6 November) he polled 11,705,256 votes

*See Aneurin Bevan, *Why Not Trust the Tories?* London: Gollancz, 1944, pp. 87–9.

in the last free elections to be held in the Weimar Republic. In early 1933 there was a marked swing in public sentiment away from the Nazis. So much so that Social Democrats and Conservatives alike were jubilant when Hindenburg dissolved the Reichstag and ordered new Elections for 5 March. But on 27 February the Reichstag went up in flames. The following day Hindenburg suspended the constitution, leaving the Nazis, who had an insufficient majority in the Reichstag to govern effectively, free to impose government by whip, firearms and jackboot.

NOTE 2

I mean here no direct part. Of course working-class movements and struggles profoundly affected Parliament, but the influence was indirect. The personal composition of Parliament was not influenced by them. It is with the impact of a new type of Member upon Parliament that I am here dealing.

NOTE 3

The Parliamentary Secretaries' Branch of the Clerical and Administrative Workers' Union is negotiating at the time of writing for an increase in salary from £364 to £390 a year. A Member of Parliament is paid £1,000 a year, less income tax, from which he must meet all public as well as personal and family expenditures.* Most M.P.s have to budget for hotel accommodation in London when Parliament is sitting, in addition to maintaining their private households. It will therefore be apparent that unless they have some other source of income they cannot afford secretarial help.

---

* Since 1957, he is allowed a tax free allowance of £750 per annum.

2

The Role of the Legislature—
Active or Passive?

SOCIETY is not a protean mass moulded by dominant ideas, but rather a living organism absorbing ideas, giving varying degrees of vitality to some and rejecting others completely. The ideas that occur to the minds of men, and the objective reality to which we attempt to relate them, are separate entities only for the purpose of study. In fact they are two parts of a single whole, each acting on the other, and what emerges from the interaction is not easy to predict. What the practitioner in social action should say to himself is: 'I know what I want to do and what I am trying to do, but what I have actually done I shall not know until I have done it.'

This, however, does not exempt us from attempting to predict and to influence the course of events, for the vitality of our own ideas and the fidelity with which we try to achieve them are themselves active forces in the flux of things. The influence of ideas on social events is profound, and is not less so because things turn out differently from what we expect. Disillusionment is a bitter fruit reaped only by the intellectually arrogant.

Between the myopic attitude of the purely 'practical man' and that of the 'intellectual', who sees society merely in terms of ideas, lies a fertile terrain ready to be cultivated by all who are prepared to recognize that political intentions are secular, always limited, but nevertheless frequently dynamic. Like the tools of other crafts, they are blunted in use and may have to be renovated and sometimes discarded for others more apt.

This secular, transitory, limited and provisional nature of political institutions and ideas is sometimes taken as an excuse for a tepid faith and an inconstant application, as though only the eternal and the absolute should command our enthusiasm. The history of human endeavour, and of science, as disciplined endeavour, would indeed be a woeful history of failure if that were the case. It is the finished work, and not the tools of his craft, that excites the love of the artist. It is the sum of human achievement and the enlargement and growing urbanity of the lives of individual men and women that should reinforce the constancy of the political practitioner if he is to be worthy of his cause.

The student of politics must therefore seek neither universality nor immortality for his ideas and for the institutions through which he hopes to express them. What he must seek is integrity and vitality. His Holy Grail is the living truth, knowing that being alive the truth must change. If he does not cherish integrity then he will see in the change an excuse for opportunism, and so will exchange the inspiration of the pioneer for the reward of the lackey.

He must also be on his guard against the old words, for the words persist when the reality that lay behind them has changed. It is inherent in our intellectual activity that we seek to imprison reality in our description of it. Soon, long before we realize it, it is we who become the prisoners of the description. From that point on, our ideas degenerate into a kind of folklore which we pass to each other, fondly thinking we are still talking of the reality around us.

Thus we talk of free enterprise, of capitalist society, of the rights of free association, of parliamentary government, as though all these words stand for the same things they formerly did. Social institutions are what they do, not necessarily what we say they do. It is the verb that matters, not the noun.

If this is not understood, we become symbol worshippers. The categories we once evolved and which were the tools we used in our intercourse with reality become hopelessly blunted. In these circumstances the social and political realities we are supposed to be grappling with change and reshape themselves independently of the collective impact of our ideas. We become the creature and no longer the partner of social realities. As we fumble with outworn categories our political vitality is sucked away and we stumble from one situation to another, without chart, without compass, and with the steering-wheel lashed to a course we are no longer following.

This is the real point of danger for a political party and for the leaders and thinkers who inspire it. For if they are out of touch with reality, the masses are not. Indeed, they are reality. For them their daily work is an inescapable imperative. While those who are supposed to be doing the theorizing for them are adrift like passengers in an escaped balloon, the workers are tied to reality by the nature of their work. In the absence of clear theoretical guidance they make empirical adaptations and formulate practical categories. So far as these are incomplete, and therefore unsatisfactory, the first result is a distrust of those who have demonstrably failed them.

The first function of a political leader is advocacy. It is he who must make articulate the wants, the frustration, and the aspiration of the masses. Their hearts must be moved by his words, and so his words must be attuned to their realities. If he speaks in the old false categories they listen at first and nod their heads, for they hear a familiar echo from the past. But if he persists, they begin to appreciate that he is no longer with them. He is not their representative any longer in the true meaning of that much abused term.

A representative person is one who will act in a given situation in much the same way as those he represents would act in that same situation. In short, he must be of their kind. They may not know the facts as he knows them. Indeed, they cannot expect to do so. In our complicated society there must be division of labour, but that division will operate in an atmosphere of confidence only if those working it are of like mind. Thus a political party which begins to pick its personnel from unrepresentative types is in for trouble. Confidence declines.

Election is only one part of representation. It becomes full representation only if the elected person speaks with the authentic accents of those who elected him. That does not mean he need be provincial, nor that he speaks in the local vernacular. It does mean he should share their values; that is, be in touch with their realities.

Political parties, like individuals, can have split personalities. In fact all political parties in time develop schizophrenia. But for them, shock therapy may well prove fatal.

Politics is an art, not a science. By the study of anthropology, sociology, psychology and such elements of social and of political economy as are relevant, we try to work out correct principles to guide us in our approach to the social problems of the time. Nevertheless, the application of those principles to a given situation is an art. The failure to recognize this has caused the leaders of the Soviet Union to make blunder after blunder, not only in Russia itself but more especially in their attitude to other countries.

In particular, the significance of the new relationship between the Soviet Union and Yugoslavia deserves serious study, for here is one of the most valuable political mutations in all history.

The Soviet Union is fond of saying that the Revolution cannot be exported. Yet that is precisely what they are always trying to do. It is unnecessary to discuss here whether the Soviet leaders have adopted the only course open to them under the conditions prevailing in Russia. It is more to the point that they seem unable to appreciate that the same pattern is not everywhere applicable, even if it were desirable.

Marshal Tito explained in a speech delivered in the Yugoslav Parliament in 1948 some of the differences that had developed between Russia and Yugoslavia. During the war the partisan forces under Tito had fought for years without direct communication with the outside world, especially with the Soviet Union. Consequently they had developed their own forms of organization as well as their own ideas about the future of their country. In particular they had definite ideas about the role of the peasants.

These had fought alongside the urban workers with the greatest heroism for the deliverance of their country. For them, the war was essentially a struggle for national independence. The passionate desire for national freedom, which is the centuries-old tradition of the peoples of Yugoslavia, merged during the war with the revolutionary aims of the Yugoslav Communists. There was therefore a clear understanding between the two. For the urban workers, Socialism, for the peasants, land, and for both national independence.

But this was far from the intention of the Soviet leaders. They had developed the psychology of what Tito has described as the 'leading nation', which is a polite term for imperialism. Through the medium of the Cominform the Soviet Union wished to bind Yugoslavia to her as she had bound Poland, Rumania, Bulgaria and

Hungary. Yugoslav institutions, ideas and policies were to follow the Soviet pattern. Under no conditions could the Soviet Union accept the role intended for the Yugoslav peasants. This is clear from the correspondence that passed between the two countries. To accept the Yugoslav view would not only violate the basic principles of Stalinism, but it would also seem to reflect upon the wisdom of the Soviet's own past policy in this respect.

By insisting on her independence, Yugoslavia threw down the gauntlet to the Soviet Union. In this it challenged the most sacred thesis which has held all the Communist parties of the world in subjection to Russia. Whenever a Communist whispers a word of criticism of Soviet policy he is silenced by the slogan, 'The Soviet Union is the headquarters of the Revolution.' From this it follows that what is in her interests is in the interests of the workers everywhere. The result has been an intellectual dependence on the Soviet so complete as to amount to bondage.

Yugoslavia is the first instance of a Communist country rebelling against this dogma. China will be next. For the Yugoslav Communists the idea was intolerable. After having fought and won a struggle for national independence in which countless lives had been lost, they were asked to exchange their new-won liberty for the tutelage of the Soviet bureaucracy.

The experience of Yugoslavia in her relations with the U.S.S.R. is the most striking modern illustration of what happens when political parties apply outworn categories to different national situations and to novel situations within nations. This may seem obvious. Unfortunately the obvious is the last thing we respect, especially if it requires self-examination and self-criticism.

The Marxist school of political thought is the one most accused of arid political dogma, and indeed, being the most active in the world, it is probably the most guilty. Marx, and the school which he founded, put into the hands of the working class movement of the late nineteenth and the first part of the twentieth centuries the most complete blueprints for political action the world has ever seen. Mountains of literature have been written to prove that Marx was wrong. If that be the case, then never was error more fertile in practice. No serious student who studies the history of the last half century can deny the ferment of ideas associated with the names of Marx, Engels and Lenin. Their effectiveness in arming the minds of working class leaders all over the world with intellectual weapons showed that their teaching had an organic relationship with the political and social realities of their time.

To deny that is to shut one's eyes to what is happening around us. The opponents of Marxism are usually so deeply prejudiced that they are shut off from reality by a wall of their own making. Their unscholarly bias renders them as unfit guides to political conduct as the Marxist dogmatists. A sympathetic understanding of what Marxists are trying to say to the world is a prerequisite to learning where the Marxist practitioners are liable to go wrong.

In so far as I can be said to have had a political training at all, it has been in Marxism. As I was reaching adolescence, towards the end of the First World War, I became acquainted with the works of Eugene V. Debs and Daniel de Leon of the United States. At that time I was reading everything I could lay my hands on. Tredegar Workmen's Library was unusually well stocked with books of all kinds. When I found that the political polemics of de Leon and Debs were shared by so loved an author as Jack London, the effect on my mind was profound.

Nor was I alone in this. My experience has been shared by thousands of young men and women of the working class of Britain, and, as I have learned since, of many other parts of the world. From Jack London's *Iron Heel* to the whole world of Marxist literature was an easy and fascinating step. The relevance of what we were reading to our own industrial and political experience had all the impact of a divine revelation. Everything fell in place. The dark places were lighted up and the difficult ways made easy.

For those whose lives are a progression from preparatory school to public school and from there to a university, it is not easy to understand the process of self-education. The self-educating naturally seize on the knowledge that makes their own experience intelligible. It is not so much that they look for immediately useful knowledge. In that they are less utilitarian than the university student who has to acquire the knowledge that enables him to pass examinations. That is why, I suppose, the self-educating cling to what they learn with more tenacity than the university product. The self-educated man learns only what interests him and interest is the begetter of intelligence. As a general rule he learns only what has a significance in his own life. The abstract ideas which ignite his mind are those to which his own experience provides a reference.

Thus action and thought go hand-in-hand in reciprocal revelation. The world of concrete activity renovates, refreshes and winnows the ideas he gets in books. The world of abstract thought rises from strong foundations of realized fact, like a great tree, whose topmost leaves move in obeisance to the lightest zephyr, yet the great trunk itself issues the final command.

I must not be thought to be extolling the virtues of self-education against those of trained instruction. Trained instruction often makes for a wider mobility, both in thought and action. But what the self-educated learn they hold, and what they hold is an illumination of their own experience. As I have already said, I was especially fortunate in the quality of the library which had been built up by the pennies of the miners and given its distinctive quality by a small band of extraordinary men, themselves miners and self-educated. They made available to us both the orthodox economists and philosophers, and the Marxist source books, and thus showed a more receptive attitude and less bigotry than many of our school and college libraries at that time.

Quite early in my studies it seemed to me that classic Marxism consistently understated the role of a political democracy with a fully developed franchise. This is the case, both subjectively, as it affects the attitude of the worker to his political responsibilities, and objectively, as it affects the possibilities of his attaining power by using the franchise and parliamentary methods.

This is especially the case in a country with a fully matured parliamentary democracy like Great Britain. Of course, quotation after quotation can be produced from the works of Marx, Engels and Lenin to show their awareness of the facts of parliamentary democracy.[4] But they never developed this feature of their philosophy to anything like the extent of the rest.

The proof of this is to be found not in the documents but in the influence their teaching had on the leaders of my young days.

Parliamentary action was looked upon as an auxiliary of direct action by the industrial organizations of the workers. Power, we were taught, was at the point of production, and there we were already well organized. This attitude was fostered by the industrial power with which workers like the miners, the transport workers, and the railwaymen emerged from the 1914–1918 war. Going to Parliament seemed a roundabout and tedious way of realizing what seemed already within our grasp by more direct means. As a South Wales leader of great intellectual power and immense influence, Noah Abblet, put it, 'Why cross the river to fill the pail?' These dreams of easy success did not survive the industrial depression of the twenties. Mass unemployment was a grim school. Industrial power was just what the unemployed did not possess.

To render industry idle as a means of achieving political victory was hardly an effective weapon in such circumstances. Capitalism had already done it for us. Also, many of the most influential Labour leaders had not grasped the revolutionary implication of mass industrial action, and those who had were not prepared to accept them.

I remember vividly Robert Smillie describing to me an interview the leaders of the Triple Alliance had with David Lloyd George in 1919. The strategy of the leaders was clear. The miners under Robert Smillie, the transport workers under Robert Williams, and the National Union of Railwaymen under James Henry Thomas, formed the most formidable combination of industrial workers in the history of Great Britain. They had agreed on the demands that were to be made on the employers, knowing well that the government would be bound to be involved at an early stage. And so it happened. A great deal of industry was still under government wartime control and so the state power was immediately implicated.

Lloyd George sent for the Labour leaders, and they went, so Robert told me, 'truculently determined they would not be talked over by the seductive and eloquent Welshman'. At this Bob's eyes twinkled in his grave, strong face. 'He was quite frank with us from the outset,' Bob went on. 'He said to us: "Gentlemen, you have fashioned, in the Triple Alliance of the unions represented by you, a most powerful instrument. I feel bound to tell you that in our opinion we are at your mercy. The Army is disaffected and cannot be relied upon. Trouble has occurred already in a number of camps. We have just emerged from a great war and the people are eager for the reward of their sacrifices, and we are in no position to satisfy them. In these circumstances, if you carry out your threat and strike, then you will defeat us.

' "But if you do so," went on Mr Lloyd George, "have you weighed the consequences? The strike will be in defiance of the government of the country and by its very success will precipitate a constitutional crisis of the first importance. For, if a force arises in the state which is stronger than the state itself, then it must be ready to take on the functions of the state, or withdraw and accept the authority of the state. Gentlemen," asked the Prime Minister quietly, "have you considered, and if you have, are you ready?" From that moment on,' said Robert Smillie, 'we were beaten and we knew we were.'

After this the General Strike of 1926 was really an anticlimax. The essential argument had been deployed in 1919. But the leaders in 1926 were in no better theoretical position to face it. They had never worked out the revolutionary implications of direct action on such a scale. Nor were they anxious to do so. Industrial action was in the air and they could not deny it. The General Election of 1918 had been a cheat, and the majority in the House of Commons did not represent the post-election mood of the country. Nevertheless, the authority of Parliament is part of the social and political climate of Britain, and it was so even in the days when the House of Commons was elected on a more limited franchise than today.

It was not so much the coercive power of the state that restrained the full use of the workers' industrial power. That is a typical error of the undeveloped Marxist shool. The incident I have described illustrates that. The workers and their leaders paused even when their coercive power was greater than that of the state. The explanation must be sought in the subjective attitude of the people to the existence of the franchise and all that flows from it. The opportunity for power is not enough if the will to seize it is absent, and that will is attendant upon the traditional attitude of the people

B*

towards the political institutions that form part of their historical heritage.

Even as a very young man, when I was studying Marxism, I was deeply conscious of this failure to take account of what, for want of a better phrase, I call the subjective attitude of peoples. It is certainly more responsible than anything else for the failure of the Communists of Great Britain to win a substantial following among the workers.

The classic principles of Marxism were developed when political democracy was as yet in its infancy. The state was a naked instrument of coercion, accompanied by varying degrees of royal absolutism. Great inequalities in the distribution of wealth, with the spectacle of degrading poverty at the bottom and ostentatious expenditure at the top of the social scale, were rendered possible only by class domination. All improvements in the condition of the masses resulted from three influences: genuine sympathy, and the philanthropy flowing from it, as in the case of the Earl of Shaftesbury; ameliorative measures, partly actuated by decency and partly by the fear of social unrest; and, thirdly, the necessity to educate the masses in the techniques of modern production methods.

In each case it was inevitable that the initiative came from the top, because the lower stratum of society was politically inarticulate. Progress lacked the thrust which comes from the people when they are furnished with all the institutions of a fully developed political democracy. The theory of the class struggle and the conception of the state, as the executive instrument of the ruling class, was an inevitable outcome of such a situation. It was the only answer conceivable to the principles of authoritarianism implicit in society, and often made explicit in the arguments of the apologists of the day. In the absence of political freedom, civil war and revolution remained the only hope of emancipation for the masses, and still must appear to be the only hope where similar conditions exist. You can rule either by counting heads or by breaking them. The ruling cliques of Britain did not hesitate to break heads when they deemed it necessary as at Peterloo, at Newport and in the case of the Tolpuddle martyrs.

Of course, stability can be maintained when political liberty is enlarged and economic conditions improved at a pace that is acceptable to the masses. This is the case in many of the British colonies. The acceleration of the pace which has occurred in recent years is one of the proudest achievements of the Labour government in Britain. Political and economic exploitation is resented with supercharged bitterness when it occurs at the hands of a foreign power, for then the emotions of class and nation merge.

In the main, stability was maintained in Britain during the latter part of the nineteenth century, despite frequent industrial unrest, because social improvements and an expansion of the franchise eased the tensions and offered the hope of still further improvement in the lot of the masses. These tensions were further cushioned by colonial exploitation and purged by emigration. The festering sores of Europe suppurated into the New World.[5]

Without emigration it is not easy to see how revolution could have been avoided. Even in Britain the easement afforded by it was considerable. During the bad years the emigration officer was busy in South Wales, Scotland, Lancashire and Durham, indeed, in every place where unemployment tugged at local roots.

I recall one incident vividly. In parts of Monmouthshire whole townships were idle for years. The poverty was appalling and the outlook black to the point of despair. The Parliament of business men elected after the 1914–1918 war looked on helplessly, while the craft skills acquired over generations of industrial expansion rusted and rotted. Idle looms, deserted pits and silent steelworks mocked at the claims of capitalist economics. What was the advice offered the workers? If there are deserted pits in Britain, sink more in Australia. If there is no use for steel in the old world, make more in the new. If Welsh miners are not allowed to dig coal for Lancashire weavers, and the weavers must not make shirts for Welsh miners, then go abroad and repeat the same monstrous muddle elsewhere. At the same time London's financial houses were providing credit for the export of modern textile machines to India. By the alchemy of capitalist finance, Bombay had been brought nearer to London than Bradford.

In the meantime the unemployed miners marched. In my district they marched first to the Board of Guardians for poor law relief.

As this was in the beginning provided from the local rates the
situation was ridiculous, for of course unemployed miners could not
pay rates with which to relieve themselves. In these circumstances
the Guardians applied to Whitehall for grants.[6] These were refused,
but loans were offered on condition that the scales of relief were cut.
Mr Chamberlain insisted on this, because for him Bedwellty was as
far away as later Czechoslovakia became.

The conditions demanded by Whitehall were unacceptable to the
unemployed, for they involved semi-starvation. So the unemployed
marched on the workhouse at Tredegar where the Guardians were
meeting. They marched from Tredegar, Ebbw Vale, Nantyglo and
Blaina, and I marched with them – at the head of them – for I was
one of the leaders. And we locked the Guardians in for two days
and nights. Nor were the Guardians annoyed with us, for they were
in the main our own people. They were one with us in our attitude
to the parsimony of Whitehall.

As the siege of the workhouse continued we held innumerable
discussions with each other about the outlook for the future. One
of the leaders was a man from Blaina. He was as fine a man as I have
ever known. Intelligent, well read, and entirely self-educated, he
was one of the best of the finest generation of workers that Britain
has ever produced. We were standing in the workhouse yard
watching the guard we had set up outside the main building. It was
a lovely day. The white clouds were drifting across a high blue sky.
The hills lifted towards the rim of the Black Mountains, faintly
etched in the far distance.

'Aneurin,' he said to me, and to this day I can hear the sad under-
tones of his voice, 'this country is finished. Come with me to
Australia. I've sold my house and I can just manage to pay my debts
and make the passage money. My house cost me six hundred pounds.
They gave me one hundred and fifty for it. There's no hope for us
here. You and I between us can do better for ourselves in a new
country than here, where all that seems left to us is to rot in idleness.'

His words moved me profoundly, for he was a man for whom I
had an affection amounting to love, and I felt my eyes flooding. For
a while I said nothing, for I wished to be clear about my own position, and I hated saying anything that might hurt him. Then I

replied. 'David,' I said, 'I hate to see you leave us, but if this is how you feel about it then you must go and I wish you all the luck in the world. For myself, I'm going to stay here and fight it out. You're an older man than I am, and you've lost your home, and it must seem too difficult to go on living here with the old memories. But if all the young men leave, who is to continue the fight, and I can't bear the thought of seeing them win over us.' I said this in no spirit of braggadocio, for all my impulses were to go with him.

When I returned home and told my father of our conversation he said, 'I think you've made the right decision, but it will be a long fight.'

He himself did not live long to see the fortunes of the struggle. He died in my arms in 1925, choked to death by pneumoconiosis. No compensation was paid him by the mine owners; in those days it was not scheduled as an industrial disease under the Workmen's Compensation Acts.

I hope the reader will not find this too long a digression from the argument. It is intended as a personal illustration of the price good men have paid for evil policies and of how the ruling cliques of Britain relieved themselves of their victims.

With the collapse of the General Strike in 1926, the workers of Britain seemed to have exhausted the possibilities of mass industrial action. As I have pointed out, the trade union leaders were theoretically unprepared for the implications involved. They had forged a revolutionary weapon without having a revolutionary intention. The miners fought on, hoping to rescue tolerable conditions from the disaster. Month after month they kept up the struggle against every device the mine owners, helped by a Conservative government, could bring to bear.

But their position was hopeless. The British governing class was determined to crush their resistance at whatever cost. And the cost was high. We are still paying it.

During the whole episode I was acutely aware of the significance of what was occurring. Not only had I the knowledge of what Robert Smillie had said to me, to cast a sombre light on the tragedy, but I was a delegate to all the conferences of the miners, and I spent much time in the company of A. J. Cook, the miners' national secretary. Arthur Cook has come in for more than his share of blame for the events of 1926. Certainly he had his faults. His evangelical zeal was greater than his negotiating skill, but he was passionately devoted to the miners, and he burned himself out in a flame of protest against the unjust conditions imposed on his people.

To me the events of that time had an eerie character. It was like watching a film unfold that I had already seen made. The currents of history were running strongly against us and in the result we were sucked under.

The defeat of the miners ended a phase, and from then on the pendulum swung sharply to political action. It seemed to us that we must try to regain in Parliament what we had lost on the industrial battlefield. When, therefore, in 1929, Labour was returned as the largest single party in the state, I went to the House of Commons in a mood of expectancy, but, I must confess, also with misgivings. I had little confidence in MacDonald, Snowden and Thomas. They had as little appreciation of the issues involved on the political field as had the trade union leaders on the industrial.

The Conservative Party under the leadership of Mr Stanley Baldwin was much more aware of the implications of the situation than was the Labour Party. Mr Baldwin told a friend of mine at the time that he conceived it to be his chief task to 'instruct the new arrivals in the limitations of parliamentary government'. The minority Labour government of 1924 had been a rehearsal, and from it the Conservatives had learned more than the Socialists. The Conservatives had learned that short of being in power themselves the next best thing was a Socialist government without a parliamentary majority. In these circumstances the Socialists accepted responsibility for conditions they had no real power to change.

Responsibility without power is the most dangerous of all situations for a political party with progressive pretensions. The people are more conscious of the responsibility than they are of the lack of power. Their attitude is summed up simply in the crude, but salutary slogan, 'get on or get out'.

In his management of delicate parliamentary situations Mr Baldwin was more subtle than is Mr Churchill. In 1929, when the General Election returned a stronger but still a minority Parliamentary Labour Party, Mr Baldwin did what he had done so successfully in 1924. He sat down and waited. 'Give them a chance,' he said, knowing well this was precisely what they didn't have! Mr Baldwin was a past master in the use of political inertia. He waited for Mr MacDonald to weaken his government by policies which offered a series of rhetorical gestures in place of effective action. Then, when the time came, he struck with remorseless and deadly precision.

Because of his restraint and apparent laziness, Mr Churchill called Mr Baldwin a 'power miser'. But this was a superficial appreciation of the subtlety of Baldwin's mind. I rate him very high indeed in the ranks of Conservative Prime Ministers. It is true that he presided over a period of capitalist decline in Britain. But there was no capitalist way of preventing the decline. The most that can be said against Mr Baldwin is that being a Conservative he could not get out of his economic dilemma by applying Socialist policies.

In contrast with Baldwin, MacDonald was a pitiful strategist. Instead of putting forward bold and imaginative proposals to deal with the economic and financial crisis he waited like Micawber for 'something to turn up'. It was eventually Mr Baldwin who turned up by kicking Mr MacDonald into the premiership of a so-called National Government in which MacDonald was the ignominious prisoner of a Conservative majority.

In 1930, Mr MacDonald, the alleged enemy of capitalism, was waiting anxiously for capitalism to solve its own crisis, and therefore rescue him from his embarrassments.

I remember an argument I had with him at the time. I had put down a resolution for discussion at the Parliamentary Labour Party meeting, calling attention to the impending financial crisis, and asking for a special national conference of the party to be called. Before the resolution was discussed MacDonald sent for me. At this interview he asked me to withdraw the resolution, because it was an embarrassment to the party. In the course of our conversation he told me that his economic advisers considered the crisis had reached its peak, and that we could confidently look forward to an improvement in the unemployment figures, and when this had gone far enough we could go to the country with every prospect of success. 'Recovery is just around the corner,' he said. It never seemed to occur to him that it was our business to grapple with the crisis ourselves, and that if Socialism had no remedy for a crisis in capitalism, then we had no political territory to stand on. He waved this aside as a purely theoretical attitude.

Needless to say I did not withdraw the resolution, and at the subsequent meeting was overwhelmingly defeated amidst the general rejoicing of colleagues who, a few months later, received at the hands of their constituents the lesson they had refused to learn at Westminster. I wish I could believe the lesson has yet been learned.

Just as the Industrial Revolution made Great Britain the classic place for the study of modern capitalism, so the present makes Britain the classic country in which to study the action and interaction of free democratic institutions in their relationship to the transition from capitalism to Socialism. Some might say the United States is the place, but this I would contest. The attitude of the people of the United States to their Congress is not that of the British people to the House of Commons. The American does not look to Congress for initiative in economic affairs as the Briton looks to Parliament. When a sudden demand for collective action occurs in the United States, the American business man steps in and takes charge of the government apparatus.

In time of war the British business man is mobilized in the government machine. But the difference is just there. In Britain the business man is mobilized. In the States he mobilizes. Also the nationalization of several of the great industries puts at the disposal of the British government a large number of administrators and technicians who are already part of the state apparatus. Indeed, the assimilation of this new body of quasi-civil servants constitutes the most fascinating as well as one of the most pivotal problems in Britain. The dangers arising from the existence of so important a body of bureaucrats have to be faced and resolved before we can say that we have found the right answer. But this is for discussion in another chapter.

It is essential to be clear about the role of Parliament in times of social upheaval and change if democratic processes are to be refreshed and strengthened, even as the changes are being carried out.

There is one situation which is fatal for a democratic Parliament:

that is helplessness in face of economic difficulties. At first this may seem trite. But it is just the lesson the Labour Party in Britain did not learn in 1924, nor again in 1929, and it is by no means clear that it has even now learned it.

Parliamentary democracy is essentially government by discussion. But if discussion is not quickly followed by resolute and decisive action, then the vitality of democracy declines. If the deed follows too tardily on the word then the word turns sour.

Parliament does not 'keep the ring'. Parliament is one of the contestants in the ring. It is not above the battle. It is a weapon, and the most formidable weapon of all, in the struggle. People have no use for an institution which pretends to supreme power and then does not use it. If economic power is left in private hands, and a distressed people ask Parliament in vain for help, its authority is undermined. Its role is reduced to that of a public mourner for private economic crimes. All is talked of; nothing is done. When this condition of affairs is sustained for a long period the man of action steps on to the political stage. Hitler was the prototype. Discussion and thought are associated together. If they prove inconclusive, dilatory, and vacillating, then the 'man who thinks with his blood' appears, and the worst of all demagogies emerges, the demagogy of leaderology.

This is the real crisis in democracy. People have no use for a freedom which cheats them of redress. If confidence in political democracy is to be sustained, political freedom must arm itself with economic power. Private property in the main sources of production and distribution endangers political liberty, for it leaves Parliament with responsibility and property with power. No one with experience of the House of Commons could deny that. When in office the Conservatives reduce parliamentary intervention in economic processes to a minimum. A striking instance of this was Neville Chamberlain's insistence that he had not promised at election time to deal with unemployment. It was alien to his way of thinking.

Nor, as we have seen, was he fundamentally different in this from Labour leaders of the type of Snowden and MacDonald. They did not look upon parliamentary power as an instrument for transforming the economic structure of society. For them the role of Parliament was to be ameliorative, not revolutionary. If, therefore, an economic crisis blew up, they looked to parliamentary action merely as a means to ease its consequences until such time as economic forces adjusted themselves and the storm passed.

There is plenty of evidence that this attitude of mind still persists. In the White Paper on unemployment issued by the wartime Coalition government the same mood appears.[7] The economic world was to be carefully watched for signs of an approaching crisis, like the guard on a medieval tower looking anxiously for the approach of an enemy. A small, highly-trained group of economists were to be charged with this task. Their function was to keep the world of finance, trade, and commerce under constant scrutiny. When they saw the attractiveness of long-term investment decline, and the possibilities of a general fall in prices appear, public investment was to be stimulated and various other measures taken to increase the purchasing power of the masses. It is true this showed that something had been learned from the experience of the between-war years. The old conception that the nation could not afford increased expenditure at a time of reduced trade had given way to the new conception of stimulating trade and industry by means of budget deficits.

It is not my intention to analyse the shortcomings of this policy here. I have written about it elsewhere. I attacked the fundamental basis of it in the House of Commons when the late Mr Ernest Bevin first presented it to the House of Commons. The whole conception was based on the assumption that the Coalition was to continue after the war.

What I wish to emphasize here is that parliamentary action was still to be the handmaiden of private economic activity; was still to be after the fact. Private enterprise was still regarded, in that policy, as the dominant consideration, and the role of parliamentary action was to provide a stimulant when it looked like flagging. This is wholly opposed to Socialism, for to the Socialist, parliamentary power is to be used progressively until the main streams of economic activity are brought under public direction.

I do not wish it to be thought that I attach no importance to the role of the government as an agency for the stimulation of trade when the private sector of industry looks like developing its periodic deflationary crisis. But this must always be looked upon as second best, and not as a substitute for making over society so as to eliminate the possibilities of these crises.

It is sometimes argued that Britain is exposed to world trade movements to an extent that limits the application of Socialist policies to her own economy. This is not the case. If it had been accepted in 1945, British recovery would have been retarded if not entirely frustrated. As it was, the private interests and short-sighted views of many business men made recovery more difficult than it need have been. It was so much easier for them to supply the markets to which they had been accustomed before the war than to venture into the dollar markets where competition was more fierce and where adaptability was required to meet the unusual conditions.[8] Nevertheless, the increase in exports to, and the decline in imports from, the dollar areas showed what could be done when national planning superimposed itself on private impulses.

One of the most effective means of mobilizing British resources for British purposes was control over the exchanges. This the Labour government inherited from the war. Without it we should have been economically disarmed as we had been in 1931. Even so there were loopholes in it. A considerable contribution was made to the devaluation crisis of 1949 by illicit capital movements from the sterling area. The convertibility crisis of 1947 also showed how international finance can be used to bring pressure on unpopular governments. Free trade in money and planned importing and exporting of goods won't work together.

Autarchy we cannot achieve, especially in Britain, but that does not mean that our own economic life must beat to the pulse of world commerce. We cannot insulate ourselves, but we can cushion the shocks. Also we have found that our very dependence on world supplies can be made to work to our advantage. It makes our market too valuable to other countries for them to ignore our wishes. So our buying power can be, and has been, used to fit in our purchases with our over-all needs.

One more reflection to round off the discussion about the attitude of Socialists to the use of parliamentary power. The attainment of a Socialist majority in Parliament is accompanied by a grave double responsibility; first for the success of their own claims, and second for the prestige of parliamentary action. Other parties do not assert the wisdom of collective action through Parliament as the core of their creed. At the most they ascribe to Parliament the function of assembling the conditions in which private initiative can operate most fruitfully. To that extent they have not pledged the authority of Parliament in the outcome of their plans.

With the Socialist it is otherwise. From the outset he asserts the efficacy of state action and of collective policies. His failure is the failure of parliamentary initiative. If that happens, where can the anxious citizen turn? Back to private enterprise, which has already failed him? This is a dangerous dilemma full of sinister possibilities for democratic institutions. The Socialist dare not invoke the authority of Parliament in meeting economic difficulties unless he is prepared to exhaust its possibilities. If he does not, if he acts nervelessly, without vigour, ingenuity and self-confidence, then it is upon him and his that the consequences will alight. He will have played his last card and lost, and in the loss, parliamentary institutions themselves may be engulfed.

Boldness in words must be matched by boldness in deeds or the result will be universal *malaise*, a debilitation of the public will, and a deep lassitude spreading throughout all the organs of public administration. Audacity is the mood that should prevail among Socialists as they apply the full armament of democratic values to the problems of the times.

NOTE 4

The following extract from Friedrich Engels' Preface to the first English translation of Marx's *Capital* gives an unequivocal summary of Marx's views: 'Surely, at such a moment, the voice ought to be heard of a man whose whole theory is the result of a lifelong study of the economic history and condition of England, and whom that study led to the conclusion that, at least in Europe, England is the only country where the inevitable social revolution might be effected entirely by peaceful and legal means. He certainly never forgot to add that he hardly expected the

English ruling classes to submit, without a "pro-slavery rebellion", to this peaceful and legal revolution.' Karl Marx, *Capital* (Everyman's Edition), New York: Dutton, 1930, Vol. II, p. 887.

NOTE 5
In Britain, from 1881 to 1891, the net annual loss by migration averaged 2,600 persons per million of population – a rate of 77,000–86,000 per annum over the ten-year period. The main recipient was the United States which, during the hundred years 1821–1921, was reinforced by a flow of population from Europe not far short of 30 million. In 1929 Britain's net loss of population due to emigration was 76,000 persons.

NOTE 6
    'No matter how big the deputation which comes from Liverpool and other northern cities and towns to Downing Street, the Ministry of Health, or the Ministry of Labour, to complain of the expense of maintaining the local poor, it is unlikely that any action will be taken or even promised. All proposals have in effect meant that Brighton, Bournemouth and other rich towns should be asked to pay part of the cost of maintaining the poor in Liverpool and Manchester. The Government objection is that if money is to be taken from towns in the South of England to relieve rates in the North, the incentive to economy and strict administration, it is felt, would be weakened.' The *Daily Mail* in February, 1933.

One of the deputations, from Liverpool, succeeded in making its views clear to Sir Hilton Young, then Conservative Minister of Health. He is reported, in the same edition of the *Daily Mail*, as saying that 'he was glad to have been informed personally of the situation in Liverpool. He trusted, however, that the Corporation would give attention to the possibilities of securing economies in their administration.'

NOTE 7
    'In the transition period . . . employment policy will be primarily concerned with the transfer of men and women to peace-time jobs. But however smoothly this transition can be made, and however rapid may be the return to normal conditions, there will still remain for

treatment those long-term problems connected with the maintenance of an adequate and steady volume of employment which eluded solution before the war.' *Employment Policy* Cmd. 6527 H.M.S.O., May, 1944.

NOTE 8

Taking an index of 100 as representing the volume of Britain's exports in 1938, her export achievements since the war have been as follows:

					1951	
1946	*1947*	*1948*	*1949*	*1960*	*Jan.–Mar.*	*Apr.–June*
91	99	126	139	160	158	171

It should however be noted that endeavours by the government to induce British privately owned industries to export more goods to the dollar area have not been quite so successful. The figures showing the value of Britain's dollar exports in comparison with her total exports are (in millions of pounds):

	1946	*1947*	*1948*	*1949*	*1950*	*1951* (first 6 months)
	£m	£m	£m	£m	£m	£m
Exports and re-exports (f.o.b.) to the dollar area[a]	98	127	191	189	316	189
Total exports and re-exports (f.o.b.) [a]	905	1135	1588	1818	2223	1305
Percentage of dollar exports to total exports	10.8	11.2	12.6	10.4	14.2	14.4

[a] These figures have been taken from the White Papers, *United Kingdom Balance of Payments, 1946 to 1950.* Cmd. 8065, H.M.S.O., 1950; and *United Kingdom Balance of Payments, 1948 to 1951*, Cmd. 8379, H.M.S.O. 1951.

It is thus clear that although dollar exports shared in the general export expansion there was no substantial shift in the proportion going to the dollar area. The apparent increase in 1950 is largely due to the monetary advantage gained by Britain following the devaluation of the pound in 1949.

The reasons for this failure to secure a substantial diversion of our export efforts towards the dollar area were put pretty pungently in the *Board of Trade Journal* (15 October, 1949) by J. Paterson, the United Kingdom Trade Commissioner in Montreal. Speaking of our trade with Canada he said:

'Failure to appreciate that the prime responsibility for sales rests upon the manufacturer himself has been the main cause of the United Kingdom's inability to secure a greater share of the Canadian market for imported goods . . . The consensus of opinion amongst United Kingdom manufacturers resident in Canada is that attempts to influence home factories in ways and means to maintain or increase business from Canada have for the most part proved ineffective.'

3

Modern Man and Modern Society

BEFORE the rise of modern industrialism it could be said that the main task of man was to build a home for himself in nature. Since then the outstanding task for the individual man is to build a home for himself in society. I do not pretend that this definition has any sociological validity. I do claim that it is useful in enabling us to study widely differing experiences in the history of mankind.

Before the Industrial Revolution, man's relations with physical nature were immediate and direct. Agriculture was the dominant occupation, with all that is implied by that – and more is implied by it than most of us are able to appreciate. The first implication is that the individual was surrounded by few man-made things. And most of those things were demonstrably created in the struggle with the forces of nature. The social unit in which he normally lived was so small and simple that he could comprehend it within a casual stroll. Social relations were seen as personal relations, for almost all the social institutions that bore upon his life were represented by people to whom he could give a personal name. In these circumstances a phrase like the existence of 'social forces' could not possibly rise spontaneously to his mind. If the social institutions were inimical to him he never really saw them as such but rather as the malignity of the individuals dominating them. Today this is seen in the case of small-scale production where the personal relations between employer and worker obscure the property element. It is of no importance for the argument whether this is good or bad, desirable or undesirable. It is enough that it is so.

In this context the individual man was on top of his society and physical nature ruled over all. The physical elements were the main source of his sorrows as of his joys. Religion was the source of his consolation and of his terrors and one of the chief offices of the priest was not only to reconcile man with his gods but also to influence the forces of nature in his favour. Floods, famines, fires, crop failures, earthquakes, the majestic immensity of the heavens and the overpowering violence of storms, all drove home the lesson that, by comparison, he was a pygmy grudgingly permitted a brief life, a fleeting smile and then oblivion.

In these circumstances the social organism was an instrument forged by man to hold in check the forces of nature. It was as much a tool evolved in the struggle for existence as the hoe with which he tilled the fields and the weapons with which he hunted wild animals or other men. The individual and society were not only inseparable from each other but it would never occur to him that it could be otherwise. Exile was death, physical and spiritual. Between him and the terrors of nature stood only his tribe, his clan, his small society. Inside it he was warm, comforted, and to some extent safe. Outside he was nothing.

I have dwelt at some length on what may appear to be such obvious facts in order to point the differences between that situation and ours. The difference is so great that it is one of kind as well as of degree. The individual today in the industrial nations is essentially an urban product. He is first a creature of his society and only secondarily of nature.

It is true he is more detached from society than were his fore-runners, but he is less detached in the sense that today the forces that control his life are man-made. Society has won a place for him in the framework of nature, but in the doing of it the social environment is the one that has become 'natural' to him. He is now surrounded by man-made things and nature has been pushed back and at the same time tamed. The physical sciences have triumphed to such a degree that the ancient sources of terror have almost ceased to preoccupy his psyche. Wherever he looks the achievements of his own hands are apparent; and he is conscious of the fact that this is only a beginning. Science promises even more than it has yet achieved, and if what it promises looks somewhat ominous, it serves to emphasize the same point – it will be man-made and not nature-made. In short, man in making society has brought nature under control. But in doing so society itself has got out of the control of man.

Now, the vicissitudes that afflict the individual have their source in society. It is this situation that has given currency to the phrase 'social forces'. Personal relations have given way to impersonal ones. The Great Society has arrived and the task of our generation is to bring it under control. The study of how it is to be done is the function of politics.

I started this chapter by saying that the problem for man is now how to make a home for himself in society. To discover what is meant by this, let us ask ourselves what it is that science has been trying to do for us in respect of the forces of physical nature. It has been trying to make them predictable, to learn how they behave, and, by anticipating their behaviour, to control them to our uses. Science therefore seeks certainty, not adventure. Indeed, it might be said that the adventure of science is to realize the greatest degree of certainty. Science does not scrap the textbooks so that each generation can start the adventure of finding out anew. It piles up a corpus of reasonably exact knowledge within which it can move with a sure touch on the periphery of the uncharted. It does not claim that its search is for the absolutely predictable. But it does claim that the more predictable the better.

If, therefore, individual man is to make a home for himself in the Great Society, he must also seek to make the behaviour of social forces reasonably predictable. The assertion of anti-Socialists that private economic adventure is a desirable condition stamps them as profoundly unscientific. You can make your home the base for your adventures, but it is absurd to make the base itself an adventure. Yet this is the claim made by anti-Socialists. The digging for coal, the making of steel, the provision of finance, the generation and distribution of electricity, the building and siting of factories and houses, the whole complete structure of the Great Society is, for the anti-Socialist, a great arena for private economic adventure. The greater the degree of unpredictability the greater the adventure, and, in theory at least, the more precious the prizes. That is why anti-Socialists shudder at the very name of planning and why planners and planning are the daily butt of reactionary newspapers.

Nor is this difficult to understand. Their principal proprietors made their fortunes not by owning newspapers (these they bought to protect their fortunes and enlarge their personal power), but by successful speculation in industry and finance. They lay in wait for the unwary and then leapt upon them from the financial undergrowth. They are pouncers, not planners.

For the great mass of the people the case is wholly different. They are the victims who are preyed upon. It is they who are stalked and waylaid, harried and tormented, their lives made a nightmare of uncertainty. To the extent that this is no longer so in Britain and in some other advanced countries, it is because the economic adventurers have been curbed and controlled in one sphere of social activity after another. Life has been made more tolerable by their defeat, not by their ascendancy.

It would be historically inaccurate to underestimate the part that private economic adventure has played in bringing modern industrial techniques into existence. The stimulus of competition, the appetite for profits, and the urge for wealth and power and status – all these played their part in the making of modern society. It may be we could have reached here by other methods and more seemly incentives. It is now idle to speculate. That was the road mankind took, and we have to deal with what he has created in taking it. We look back along the roadway to see the direction taken, not so much to condemn the road makers, but because it is essential to comprehend the nature of what we have created if we are to make our way in the new environment.

The methods that were adopted in the making of the Great Society have little application to its present management. Nor does history furnish us with any lessons, for we have not passed this way before. In so far as past civilizations contained an urban element, it was merely a fringe to the vast hinterland where agricultural pursuits imposed a primitive pattern on the majority of mankind. The continuity of civilization is essentially the by-product of its urban culture. Where the division of labour between town and country permitted a surplus of food, the products of the mind appeared and commerce quickened still further the explorations of the intellect.

All the great teachers of the past arose at this stage. Urban crafts, and the culture dependent on them, enabled a few elevated minds to speculate on man's destiny and on the nature of life and things. But luminous though these speculations were, their influence was comparatively limited, for the vast majority of mankind could not lift their heads long enough from the primitive hoe and plough for their minds to be ignited.

One of the most fascinating sidelights on the story of mankind is the gulf which persisted between urban illumination and the twilight behind. All ancient civilization bears testimony to this truth. The countryside was earth-bound, and so little did it share the intellectual excitement of the urban fringe that between the two there has always been hostility. The country was exploited by the town and could not share in what the town could give it: the magic of intellectual speculation, the thrill of newly awakened beauty in the hands of the craftsman obeying the inspiration of the artist, and the yearning of the explorer for new lands and strange experience. The labour of the country dweller fertilized the life of the town, but he was shut out from its excitements. Country labour was too hard for leisure, and without leisure the mind remained torpid.

Where the countryside is neglected it always takes its revenge. Unless country and town march together in reciprocal activity, civilization will limp on one foot. This lesson we in Britain are learning. There are some nations that have not done so. The failure of the Soviet Union in this respect may yet prove fatal to the regime.

The British have no right to be complacent about the way the countryside has been treated, and if, as a consequence, the British people have not suffered more than they have, it is because history has favoured us in this as in so many other ways. We enjoyed advantages denied to some of the agrarian countries on which Western civilization is now making its full impact, with consequences for mankind that still remain to be unfolded. For more than a century British merchants, and the squirearchy, had been accumulating innumerable pools of capital, and when these were flushed by freshets from the maritime discoveries, sufficient capital was at hand to launch the Industrial Revolution.

Even so the sufferings of the workers, both rural and urban, have to be studied to be believed. It is not necessary to describe them here for they have been dealt with by Friedrich Engels, the two Hammonds, Arnold Toynbee, and many other writers.[9] The merciless exploitation which formed the basis of the unprecedented accumulation of capital equipment in Britain was made possible only by a class dictatorship. The rate of capital accumulation was an expression of the denial of consumption goods to the masses of the people. It brooks no contradiction that if political democracy had existed at the time, the rate of capital accumulation would have been much slower.

I know the reply that will be made to this. I shall be told my argument proves that a rapid rate of economic progress is inconsistent with the existence of the universal franchise. This is true of backward communities where the agricultural population is able to produce only small surpluses over and above what is needed for its own reproduction. But what conclusion must we draw from that? What is the use of taunting the underdeveloped countries with the absence of democratic institutions if these can survive only by a slower rate of economic progress or by help from outside? When we were at their economic level we were hanging children and driving them into the mines and into the mills and organizing labour camps in the countryside. Freedom is the by-product of economic surplus. I speak here not of national independence, freedom to use one's own language, and religious liberty, although even these have often been involved in the economic struggles. I am speaking of the full panoply of political democracy which includes these liberties and others besides. It is wholly unhistorical to talk as though political liberty had no secular roots. Political liberty is the highest condition to which mankind has yet aspired, but it is a condition to which he has climbed from lowlier forms of society. It did not come because some great minds thought about it. It came because it was thought about at the time it was realizable.

These are reflections which must be present in our minds as we witness the awakening of the Orient under the impact of Western ideas. The Eastern peoples learn by means of the motion picture, the radio, from magazines and books and in innumerable other ways of the achievements of the industrial West. They yearn for similar

things for themselves, even as they are still bound on the wheel of
primordial techniques. The ferment thus created is the more active
because the East has been, and still is, in part, a centre of imperial
conquest and exploitation. Never has such explosive material been
assembled since the barbarian hordes swept down on the Mediter-
ranean civilizations.[10]

If democratic institutions are to be helped to take root in the
Orient, it can be done, not by sending professors to teach the virtues
of democratic constitutions, but by sending the means to raise their
material standards. Man must first live before he can live abundantly.

It is just here that the United Nations is falling short of its duty.
Collective action against aggressive war is certainly essential if mankind is to survive. But it is only one half of the answer. The social
revolutions of the East will overspill national boundaries and take
on the nature of aggressive acts unless their economic tensions are
eased by assistance from the West. For, I repeat, it is impossible for
them, in a tolerable period of time, to produce from their own
surpluses sufficient to build the capital equipment of a modern
industrial community. If they are left to do so they will attempt it
under the ruthless repressive instrument of police states. Russia has
gone that way and we have not yet paid the full price.

The economic function of the police state is to hold down the
consumption of the people, especially of the peasant population,
while their surplus production is drained off for the purpose of fixed
capital investment. The smaller the surplus the slower the build-up
of fixed capital, and the more repressive the measures required.
Herein lies the whole tragedy of the Soviet Union. She has been
trying to lift herself by her boot straps. In the furtherance of this
policy she has developed an extreme centralist policy. More local
responsibility would reduce the rate of accumulation because the
nearer responsibility is to the people the more it is amenable to the
people's sufferings. From this centralist policy to the creation of a
vast bureaucracy to serve the needs of the central direction is a
short and logical step. Everything is sacrificed to the requirements
of the 'Plan'.

I remember a short visit I paid to Russia in 1930; that was during
the second year of the first Five-Year-Plan. On my return I was

asked by a trade union leader of international repute what my impressions were. I said my visit had been too short to admit of any final conclusions, but one impression I had gained: whereas in Britain we were slaves to the past, in Russia they were slaves to the future. The impression formed then has been amply confirmed by subsequent developments.

Nor can Western capitalism shed itself of a measure of responsibility for this. Russia was surrounded by a wall of hostility, trade was hampered and sometimes cut off entirely. It should not be forgotten that the Conservatives won the 1924 General Election by attacking the proposal of the then Labour government to advance a loan to Russia – a loan that would have been spent in Britain and would have provided work for the unemployed of Britain as well as capital equipment for Russia. The Iron Wall that Russia afterwards built around herself was in large measure the product of the rebuffs of those years.

At the moment it looks as though the United States is going to repeat the same folly in China. The way to treat a revolution in an agrarian country is to send it agricultural machinery, so as to increase food production to the point where the agricultural surplus will permit of an easier accumulation of the industrial furniture of modern civilization. You cannot starve a national revolution into submission. You can starve it into a repressive dictatorship; you can starve it to the point where the hellish logic of the police state takes charge.

It is pertinent here to point to the different conditions under which contemporary revolutions of the East have to be carried out as distinct from those of the Americas in the late eighteenth and early nineteenth centuries. In the latter case investment flowed freely from Europe to America, and along with the investment went skilled artisans of all kinds. It is true America did not have a large peasant population, but this was a further advantage. It was an empty country and it was filled by waves of migrants from Europe; many came from backward European countries, but the advanced nations also made their contribution.

Much of the machinery reaching America took the form of involuntary gifts, for the workings of the capitalist system produced

a series of crises accompanied by bankruptcies which left much of
the exported capital equipment unencumbered by subsequent
financial claims. To this Europe added two wars partly financed by
forced sales of European assets in America.[11]

The Eastern revolutions possess no such advantages. The forms
of international investment have changed. Private international
investment is not so mobile now as it was then, and the sums, and
therefore the risks involved are greater, as the capital equipment
itself has changed its character. The machinery exported to the
New World, in the first half of the nineteenth century, was comparatively primitive compared with the modern power station,
steelworks, factory, railway and irrigation plant. In these new conditions government lending must take the place of the private
initiative of the old enterprise.

This calls for an imaginative generosity that will tax the idealism
of the developed nations. The United States of America has already
made a contribution, and to a necessarily more limited extent, so
has Great Britain. But these are woefully small compared with the
need, and of late the ability to do more has been endangered, if not
frustrated, by a rearmament programme on, in my view, an ill-
considered and unnecessarily lavish scale.

Before aid can be given to anything like an adequate extent, the
relationship of the individual citizen to the Great Society will have
to be revised. An international design which is coherent and purposive cannot be sustained by societies which are themselves anarchic
and without aim.

There are three conceptions of society now competing for the
attention of mankind: the competitive, the monolithic, and the
democratic Socialist. There is a fourth which might be called the
authoritarian society, after the fashion of Spain and Portugal, but
in a curious way these last are not genuine societies at all. They
share many of the most repulsive features of the monolithic type
without its active genius. They are frozen societies. In so far as they
are animated at all, it is by a nostalgia for a romanticized past. They
are caught and held by a kind of historical reverie in which the
active principle of progress is debilitated by a wistful desire to
recapture the fixed relationship of the grandee, the hidalgo and the

serf. In their attempts to reconstruct the values of the past they constrain the present. They represent the future refusing to be born. They reduce the functions of government to an ugly masquerade in which the poverty of their pretensions shows through the tinsel of their ornate façade. They need another Cervantes to blow them into oblivion in a gale of laughter.

That the present regime does not represent the people of Spain is shown by its failure to mobilize their energies in an effective assault on the nation's problems. As their history has shown, the Spanish people are brave, adventurous and freedom-loving. Left to themselves they would have won their way through. But their present masters were imposed upon them by the Germany of Hitler and the Italy of Mussolini, while Tory Britain pretended to hold the ring, although in fact conspiring to keep the anti-Fascists unarmed.

With the competitive society we are sufficiently familiar. We are just emerging from it, and its 'systems of make-believe', as Thorstein Veblen called them, still pervade our thinking. Its philosophy denies to the state any but the most rudimentary functions in domestic affairs. Collective action is anathema to it. It believes that good comes from leaving the individual to pursue what he considers to be his own advantage in industry and commerce, and that this must be so because people will buy from him only what they want, and at the price they are prepared to pay.

Thus individual profit is the motive, and the market the final arbiter. Competition, we are told, can be safely left to winnow out the less competent both in production and distribution. Material success, in this philosophy, is the prize awarded by society to the individual who has served it best, so the zest for profit is really a search to discover the wishes of the community. Though the motive may be selfish the general welfare is served. Liberal philosophy believed it had discovered in this principle a method whereby private acquisitiveness and the public weal were harnessed together in the most fruitful partnership yet evolved by men.

Poverty was therefore the consequence of failing to serve the community efficiently and any undue attempt to relieve it would undermine the hedonism which lay at the heart of this creed. The kiss of material wealth for the successful; the whip of poverty for the others. Fear of unemployment was the spur which compelled the worker to do his best.

From this angle unemployment benefit was regarded with suspicion because it tended to make the worker more selective in his choice of employer, and to immobilize him in districts and countries where the prospects of employment were poor. Consequently the worker must be kept in a ferment of economic uncertainty. He must regard his home, his locality, and even his country as values to which he must not attach his affections too strongly for at any moment he might have to forsake them and follow the varying rate of profit from employer to employer, from district to district, from one part of the globe to another. If the destiny of man is merely to accumulate the means of production, then there was no previous system to compare with it. It produced more changes in the two centuries of its operation than in the ten thousand years which preceded it.

But it failed in the one function by which any social system must be judged. It failed to produce a tolerable home and a reputable order of values for the individual man and woman. Its credo was too grossly materialistic and its social climate too feverish. It converted men and women into means instead of ends. They were made the creatures of the means of production instead of the masters. The price of men was merely an item in the price of things. Priority of values was lacking because no aim was intended but the vulgar one of the size of the bank balance. It was satisfied with quantity, oblivious to the fact that the quantitative measurement will pronounce as impersonally on a Shakespearean folio as on the latest product of the production line. Efficiency was its final arbiter – as though loving, laughing, worshipping, eating, the deep serenity of a happy home, the warmth of friends, the astringent revelation of new beauty, and the earth tug of local roots will ever yield to such a test.

And if I am told this is unfair, because it never presumed to provide a home for man in the widest sense, I reply that that is just what it claimed to do; it insisted that the best kind of society would emerge from its individual motivations. In the result it produced the slums, it broke up the family, it scattered friends to the distant ends of the earth, it derided the very name of beauty in the hideous townships it created, it made love furtive, and made marriage often impossible and frequently an intolerable burden, and it sundered local association by continuous redistributions of the population.

In Britain it was failing before the 1939 war even to mobilize the forces of production efficiently. Instead of material plenty, it was conspiring to create scarcity as the condition for making profits. Today it attempts to enlarge its profits by price association, cartels, trusts, resale price maintenance, and a score of other expedients, all designed to cheat the god by which it swears in its credo – competition. In short, it is attempting to enthrone industrial and commercial authoritarianism in place of the arbitrament of the market place.

The economic decadence of pre-war Britain was strikingly revealed when we faced the task of post-war reconstruction. Most of the basic industries had been geared to the acceptance of a comparatively low standard of consumption, accompanied by a permanent army of unemployed numbering about two million. The coal industry had been rescued from complete collapse by a series of statutes, all designed to eliminate, not increase, competition among the various coal companies, and to enable them to fix the price of coal at a level that would ensure continued production in high cost pits. This was also true of steel. In the case of tin plate a rigid cartel served the same purpose. Outworn techniques prevailed in the textile industry, and our electricity supplies, as we soon discovered, were utterly unable to support an all-out production programme.

These statutory protections were in complete contradiction to what the folklore of British capitalism continued to say about itself. Private competition was still extolled even as it was being eliminated from sector after sector of our economic life. Profits were still accepted as the reward of risk and the prize of efficiency, although they were now demonstrably often the perquisite of functionless ownership.

Of course there were large areas of industrial enterprise where technical discoveries and new industrial techniques showed that it was the forms of ownership and not the inventive genius of the British people that were failing.

The technical achievements of the past hundred years have produced a type of society different from any that has ever before existed,
posing novel problems for mankind. As I said at the beginning of
this chapter, it has changed the character of the adaptations the
individual has to make to his environment. His is now a struggle
with society and not with nature. The vicissitudes that now afflict
him come from what he has done in association with other men,
and not from a physical relationship with the forces of nature. The
division of labour into which he is born weaves his own life into a
series of interdependencies involving not only his own personal
surroundings, but moving in ever-widening circles until they
encompass most parts of the earth. Modern industrial society is no
longer a multiplication of a number of simple self-sufficient social
groupings, each able to detach itself from the others without damage
to itself. It is multicellular, not unicellular. Each part is connected as
though by an infinite variety of nerves with all the others, so that
separation is now a mutilation. It is similar to a physical organism,
but with this difference: that it has no head and therefore no
mechanism with which to receive and co-ordinate the vibrations.

This is so, not only between nations, but within each nation of
the *laissez-faire* type, because such a philosophy by its very nature
rejects the propriety of an *a priori* principle. There is no way of
saying how far such a society has realized the intentions of its
architects, because there was no architect and no intention. There is
only an emergent. Science works for predictability: capitalist society
is profoundly unscientific. It proceeds upon no hypotheses, because
that would imply an order of values.

This is why it is so pathetic to hear eminent scientists deplore the
failure of man to rise to the moral stature required of him if he is to
make wise use of the powers science has put in his hands. Scientists
are also citizens. What kind of society do they think should exist?
Should the profit motive serve some other value, and if so, what is
it? If material reward is accepted as the prime motivator in society
then that is an individual prompting, acting by itself and obeying
no generalized moral intention.

From time to time a generalized purpose comes to discipline the
multitude of individual strivings, like war and the preparation for it

under fear of attack, or a struggle for national independence in the case of an oppressed nation. On these occasions a moral unity informs the whole nation and the energies of the people are super-charged by the absence of inhibitions, as Wilfred Trotter has brilliantly pointed out.

It is here we come to one of the dangers lurking in the anarchy of *laissez-faire* society. The lack of a discernible order of values to give coolness to judgement and coherence to men's relations with each other and with society, gives rise to waves of primitive gregariousness. The amoral climate of the business world exposes the psyche of the individual to unreasoning compulsions inherited from the remote past.

This is one of the explanations why nationalism is so rampant when the objective facts relegate it to a minor role in human affairs. In place of the sovereignty of rational aims, the primitive herd instincts assert themselves with threatening violence. In this mood, questions that can only be settled by changing relations within the nation are handed over to the field of group emotions, where the modern witch doctor hunts out the dissidents, and the old men of the tribe mouth the senile slogans that passed for wisdom among primitive men.

It has often been said that when revolution threatens, nations go to war, but that is too simple and rationalized a view. It does not do justice to what in fact happens. I have seen the alchemy at work too often not to appreciate the intensity with which relief is sought from a threatening situation, and from the burdens of intellectual choice. It is the same impulse that makes men shout for unity when faced with the need to resolve some painful and legitimate difference of opinion.

This mood is always difficult to resist because it does not arise from a rational analysis of the problem. On the contrary, analysis is what people want to avoid because that would lay bare the divisions which led to the tensions in the first place.

In Britain the phenomenon has been seen on several occasions and it is showing itself again. It expresses itself in the demand for a national government or for a coalition and in decrying the useful-ness of political parties. As I have said, it is the peculiar product of the competitive society where the individual is reduced too often to a condition of war with society, and with his fellows, and consequently where his group impulses are violated.

The effect of gregariousness in these circumstances is to obscure the nature of the problem. The slum landlord and the slum dweller, the profit earner and the profit taker, the gambler and his victim, the economic adventurer and the advocate of co-operation, all are summoned together in group consultations and are bathed in the warm glow which is generated by their close association. In these conditions it becomes an offence to raise the issues which divide them, for this would immediately disintegrate the association which is the source of the group emotions. The enemy has then to be sought outside the group if its members are to continue to enjoy the glow of unity. From this to demonology is a short step. Something, someone, must be found against which the group can launch itself as a united entity.

Nothing does this so effectively as another nation. The generation of hate against the out-group follows naturally from the refusal to face the problems which might divide the members of the in-group. An intense nationalism, belligerent and irrational, is therefore the natural accompaniment of the competitive society. It is the price paid for the emotional collisions that are the normal conditions of the *laissez-faire* social system. It is this which gives an underlying sanction in national rivalries to the squalid aspects of commercial exploitation. Commercial greed could not commend itself if there were not this craving for group action in a society where daily struggle in all the important features of the individual life generates an abiding nostalgia for mutual co-operation. To expect international co-operation and peace between societies within which daily life is a jungle struggle for existence is not only a contradiction in terms: it is opposed to any intelligent understanding of the psychology of *laissez-faire* society.

It is this as much as economic and commercial antagonisms between nations which explains why modern industrial society fights a series of bloody wars even as the facts of international interdependence point to international co-operation as the only rational behaviour. Rational thought fights in vain against the irrational mood that is produced by the endemic economic war in industry, commerce and finance. The psychology of competition and love of peace are uneasy bedfellows. The love of peace is certainly there, but it is overwhelmed time and again by waves of mass emotion flowing from the countless millions of little and great frustrations experienced in the competitive struggle for existence.

The accumulation of material possessions is no compensation for the rupture between the individual and society that is characteristic of competitive society. Those who succeed in the struggle equally with those who fail are invaded by the universal restlessness. The virtues of contemplation and of reflection are at a discount. Aesthetic values attend upon the caprice of the financially successful. The price ticket is displayed upon the Titian and the Renoir, and they are bought more for their prospective appreciation in capital value than for their intrinsic merit. The millionaire loots the world of its artistic treasures and then buries them in his private home, where he can display them to a few choice friends whose eyes glisten with avarice rather than with appreciation of the loveliness and craftsmanship contained in them. All around there is a restless journeying but with few arrivals.

Where lies the port to which the ship would go?
Far, far ahead, is all the seaman knows.

The vulgarity which is so characteristic of modern commercial civilization has been a recurrent theme of critics from Ruskin and Morris onwards, and it is therefore not necessary to enlarge upon it here. But it is essential to realize that most of the glories of art were produced for social and not for private consumption. The skill of architect, sculptor, painter and builder-craftsman were united in the construction of public buildings where the cost counted less than the graciousness they brought to the lives of those who lived around them. At best the rich collector makes us a legacy of his accumulated treasures, in which case they are immured in museums and art galleries, where they look reproachfully down on the long processions of sightseers, who can catch, in such a context, only a small glimpse of their beauty.

Some day, under the impulse of collective action, we shall enfran-
chise the artists, by giving them our public buildings to work upon;
our bridges, our housing estates, our offices, our industrial canteens,
our factories and the municipal buildings where we house our civic
activities. It is tiresome to listen to the diatribes of some modern art
critics who bemoan the passing of the rich patron as though this must
mean the decline of art, whereas it could mean its emancipation if
the artists were restored to their proper relationship with civic life.

I had the dilemma of the artist during a transition stage in society
very much in mind when, as Minister of Health, I was responsible
for a statute[12] which enables municipal authorities to spend public
monies on educational, artistic and other allied activities. So far,
only a minute beginning has been made in the exercise of these new
powers, for many still labour under the delusion that this is something that should be left to the private patron. If that had always
been the case, Leonardo da Vinci and Michelangelo would have died
largely inarticulate.

It might be argued that the Popes, Kings, Dukes and Princes who
patronized them did so because of their private interest in the arts.
That they were so interested is beyond question; at least in many
cases. But it is also true that they disposed of the public revenues.
They were expected to spend part of these in the adornment and
furnishing of churches, the palaces in which they lived and the
public buildings where the civic life of the community was carried
on. In so far as their private caprice prevailed, it was often to the
detriment of the freedom of the artists they employed.

NOTE 9
The stark facts of life in the early nineteenth century which so shocked
these men are, perhaps, best condensed in a commentary by Arthur
Bryant (in *Pageant of England, 1840–1940*. Collins, 1941; on the
First Report of the Children's Employment Commission, published
in 1842.

'From this document it appeared that the employment of children of seven or eight years old in coal mines was almost universal. In some pits they began work at a still earlier age: a case was even recorded of a child of three. Some were employed as "trappers", others for pushing or drawing coal trucks along the pit tunnels. A trapper, who operated the ventilation doors on which the safety of the mines depended, would often spend as many as sixteen hours a day crouching in solitude in a small dark hole. "Althought this employment scarcely deserves the name of labour," ran the Royal Commission's report, "yet as the children engaged in it are commonly excluded from light and are always without companions, it would, were it not for the passing and repassing of the coal carriages, amount to solitary confinement of the worst order . . ."

' . . . Naked to the waist, and with chains drawn between their legs, the future mothers of Englishmen crawled on all fours down tunnels under the earth drawing Egyptian burdens. Women by the age of 30 were old and infirm cripples. Such labour, degrading all who engaged in it, was often accompanied by debauchery and sickening cruelty: one witness before the Commission described how he had seen a boy beaten with a pick-axe. Lord Ashley in a speech in the Commons mentioned another whose master was in the habit of thrashing him with a stick through which a nail had been driven: the child's back and loins were beaten to jelly, his arm was broken and his head covered with the mark of old wounds.'

See also Engels' *Conditions of the Working Class in* 1844.

NOTE 10
Some idea of the disparity between the standards of life obtaining in the underdeveloped countries and those enjoyed by the Western world can be appreciated by examining the following statistics. These show the consumption and production of those goods and services which are indispensable to the establishment and maintenance of civilized life as the democracies have come to understand it. India and Britain have been chosen as the examples.

C*

	Unit	Per 1,000 of population in India	in Britain
Electricity production per year	1,000 kWh.	13	1,033
Coal consumption per year	tons	80	3,884
Petrol consumption per year	tons	7.8	327
Steel consumption per year	tons	3.8	194
Cement consumption per year	tons	7.2	148
Locomotives (per million of population)	numbers	22	410
Carrying capacity of rail passenger cars	tons	10	276
Rail freight per year	1,000 ton miles	65	446

Source: *The Colombo Plan for Co-operative Economic Development in South and South-East Asia.* Cmd. 8080, H.M.S.O., 1950.

NOTE II

Although no reliable figures of this flow are available on a yearly basis some idea of its extent may be gathered from an estimate of Herbert Feis, a well-known authority on this subject, that in December 1913 accumulated foreign investment (principally European) in the United States amounted to £3,763.3 million. Of this total Britain had provided £754.6 million.

NOTE 12

The Local Government Act, 1948, provides for a facility which has not received much publicity from the British Conservative press. Section 132 provides that:

'A local authority may do, or arrange for the doing of, or contribute towards the expenses of the doing of, anything necessary or expedient for any of the following purposes, that is to say:

(a) the provision of an entertainment of any nature or of facilities for dancing;

(b) the provision of a theatre, concert hall, dance hall or other premises suitable for the giving of entertainments or the holding of dances;

(c) the maintenance of a band or orchestra;

(d) any matters incidental to the matters aforesaid, including the provision, in connexion with the giving of any entertainment or the holding of any dance, of refreshment or programmes and the advertisement of any such entertainment or dance.'

4

Private Spending v. Government Spending

THE chief characteristic of the modern competitive society is the feverish accumulation of property in private hands. The stress is on the word accumulation. In other times individuals acquired vast fortunes, but these were usually the result of transfers of already existing wealth, not the creation of new wealth. The amount of additional wealth created during a generation was trivial compared with what was inherited; and what there was to inherit consisted in the main of land. Improvements to the land in any one generation were microscopic when contrasted with the growth of capital equipment in a modern industrial nation. With the possibility of converting agricultural surplus into commodities to be bought and sold in the rapidly growing urban communities, the last link with medieval society was broken. This process, with its pressure on the rural communities to produce more and more surplus for exchange with the novel manufactured products, created new tensions between town and country.

In mid-nineteenth-century Britain the overwhelming proportion of spending was by the private citizen. Public spending was reduced to a minimum. This was implicit in the industrial situation as well as explicit in the philosophy of the time. Wealth had first to flow through the hands of the private citizen, who was expected to set aside as much of it as possible for the making of more wealth. Public spending was seen as an interference, not only with the rights of the individual, but as an enemy of the process of capital accumulation. This is still orthodox Conservative opinion.

Everything was now bought and sold, and the proceeds were invested with increasing ardour in the industries which the Industrial Revolution was calling into existence. Common spending, communal pleasures, devotion to public elegance, the adornment of cities, public building, all were seen as diversions from the all-devouring appetite to increase the possibilities of private wealth opened up by the daily discoveries of the mechanical sciences.

This is a familiar story, but its deeper significance is only now beginning to be realized. Private initiative was almost the only initiative allowed. Government was reduced to its most rudimentary form: the judiciary, and the armed forces which lay at its back.

There being nothing in the public exchequer that was not wrung from the reluctant taxpayer, communal need and private greed were in constant war with each other. The balance of power lay every time with the taxpayer because he controlled the votes that elected the government. Where this was not the case the cry 'No taxation without representation' went up. In obedience to this demand the franchise was extended. But it would be a mistake to regard this as democracy on the march, except incidentally. It was rather new wealth on its defence against invasion by public spending. It was not a demand for collective activity, but rather for its curtailment. The public domain must be restricted or it would slow down, if not stop altogether, the rate of saving, and therefore the technical progress which was seen as the main purpose of human endeavour.

There was economic justification behind this attitude. The law of the new economics was merciless. You had to get richer or you got poorer. You might have attained to a comfortable position but you could not rest there. Two factors made it impossible. In the first place there was your competitor. He might get ahead of you and push you out of the race. You had to be on the alert to learn new ideas, improved modes of production, and to secure fresh markets. One aspect of the new economic law was more potent even than that. The new machines coming along were more expensive to replace than the old. In setting aside savings regard had to be paid to that contingency. All the time you had to keep on acquiring more expensive plant or eventually you would own none. You found yourself sitting on an escalator which moved ever forwards; and you could not sit still on it; you yourself had to work the levers that made it move or you would fall off or be pushed off by others anxious to work them.

It was no wonder that the philosophers of the new order rejoiced at the situation. Apparently mankind had at last discovered a form of society in which the individual was compelled to serve the common good in satisfying his own interests. To this I have already referred. What I wish to emphasize here is the fact that society had handed over to the individual almost the entire function of looking after the accumulation of what I have called its social furniture. But unfortunately it had done it by a method that produced universal enslavement. Progressive accumulation of capital goods was now pursued for its own sake. The accumulators could not stop accumulating.

Nor could they slow down and take time to look around them to see what it was they had created. 'What is this life if full of care we have no time to stand and stare?' the Welsh tramp poet asks reproachfully. But the capitalist, bound to his ever-revolving wheel, was in no position to respond. His only compensation was that the wheel was getting bigger and bigger, and so in its revolutions he was able to stay just a little longer on top.

Thus the successful as well as the unsuccessful are unemancipated in the competitive society. The only wealth in which the entrepreneur is allowed to be interested, by the economic function allotted him, is the wealth that will lead to more wealth. Consumption for its own sake is made a function of consumption for further production. All forms of consumption which do not immediately feed the productive process are looked upon as uneconomic, as wasteful, as spendthrift. So it was thought and so it was.

But no sooner had the utilitarian principles of capitalism been universally adopted than men began to revolt against the type of society they produced. The history of the last hundred years is the story of how collective action has progressively modified the situation created by the triumph of money values. No society can long endure which fails to secure the assent of the people When we study the history of human society, especially those forms of social organization which lasted many centuries, it is difficult for us to understand how it was that men and women came not only to tolerate, but cheerfully to acquiesce in, conditions and practices which seem to us at this distance to be revolting. The answer is not the simple one that the masses were held down by sheer physical force. That is possible for a short time: but it cannot explain the continuity of centuries of the same conditions. The institutions and modes of behaviour of these societies must have, in part at least, commended themselves to ordinary men and women or they would have been undermined by sheer disapproval. Ultimately, rulers, however harsh, must share the same values as the ruled if their empires are to persist. Obedience is rendered in the last resort, and for any considerable length of time, by accepting the moral and intellectual sanctions that lie behind social compulsions. To represent the history of mankind as a record of sullen submission to alien values, at the threat of the whip, and the fear of the executioner, is to affront our intelligence as well as to offend the dignity of human beings.

Thus there must always have been compensations and amenities, pleasures and common rituals, making life seem worth while and forming the cement that bound ancient societies together in a continual reaffirmation of willing consent.

Such consent capitalist society has not been able to secure in any country where it has won a complete victory. If I am told that the United States is a rebuttal of this contention, then I answer that history has yet to pronounce the verdict on her. She has lasted too short a time to claim that the principles which dominate her life have the quality of permanence. What we are able to say is that where the same principles triumphed in the countries of Europe they have been or are being deserted and in some instances completely overthrown.

This is not difficult to understand. The record is immediately behind us for the reading. The reason for the impermanence of capitalist society consists in the fact that it is merely an accumulation of private values and these take no account of the common values that are the essential condition for social survival and continuity. Disposal of the economic surplus is a function that should belong to the sphere of collective action. It is this that a system of private economic adventure is quite unable to concede, except in the case of war and the preparation for war when group sanctions override private ambitions.

I know this will be regarded as heresy of the worst kind: and yet I must persist because in my view it lies at the heart of the modern problem. So long as the function of progressive accumulation remains the field of private initiative, the individual will never be able to make society conform to any permanently commendable pattern.

Where public spending is looked upon as an invasion of private rights, private ambitions are the enemy of any reputable system of social priorities. Even in Britain, where as much as one-fifth to one-fourth of the national income is devoted to capital investment, complaint is made all the time that the high rate of taxation is interfering with fresh investment. The complaint is not really of the rate of investment but of its direction. The demand is always that the nature of the investment as well as its amount should be left to private initiative.

The argument that public spending is at the expense of savings and therefore of new capital accumulation is subtle and persuasive. The Government is made to appear thriftless and improvident and careless of the needs of posterity. This charge is advanced, incidentally, by people whose improvidence has devastated whole provinces of their woodlands, and produced soil erosion of gigantic proportions, and who are now in the process of using up stores of precious metals so prodigally that mineralogists are raising shouts of un-heeded warnings.

Public spending is presented as an extravagance; private spending, by inference, an economy. So long as the disposal of the economic surplus is considered a function of privately inspired investment this must always be so, for private ambitions are set in conflict with public plans, and personal frustrations embitter the quarrel. Some Conservatives have carried their protests to an absurd extent. One of them, when challenged as to what public expenditure he would cut, answered 'technical education'. This shocked me at the time into calling the Conservatives 'devourers of the seed'.

Taxation, unaccompanied by selective subsidies, is not an effective instrument for remedying social inequalities except in comparatively small quantities, and gradually over long periods of time. And this for a reason that is often ignored. A sudden heavy tax that transfers purchasing power from one section of the community to another may change the pattern of consumer demand so violently as to produce a sharp rise in prices. It is true that over a period the high prices will call forth more production in the goods required. But in modern society the period can be too long, for capital is locked up in the old pattern of distribution. This is especially the case where nature fixes a rhythm that cannot be hurried, as for instance, in the production of meat and milk.

A change in consumer demand, if it is to be effected with least dislocation, should be preceded by an alteration in the direction of investment; and this is most easily done by the authority responsible for the change in the first place.

In Britain the conflict between private and public investment after the war brought into prominence the point I am here making. It illumines the difficulties that arise when social priorities are injected into a system where most of the surplus available for new investment is still privately owned. The aftermath of war left us with certain forms of investment which had prior claims on the national resources.[13] There was housing, for example, and coal mines, steelworks, and power stations, a wide variety of factories no longer adequate to the needs of a Britain in full employment: higher imports involving higher exports. It was comparatively easy to plan the public sector of our national expenditure, and to keep within the figures agreed, because public expenditure was under immediate control by Ministers and state departments. I would find myself, for instance, as Minister of Health, allotted a sum of money for such public necessities as water supplies and sewerage. I had to keep to this figure within narrow margins of at most thousands of pounds. The physical work as well as its money equivalent was well within public control, being a function of the Health Department and the local authorities. The end result was therefore predictable. But in the private sector the national plans were out by scores of millions; in commercial vehicles alone, in one year, by many millions. The explanation was that these had been produced for export but could not at the time be sold overseas. The producers could not afford to hold them and so they had to be disposed of on the domestic market.

Was this a failure of public planning? Of course not. On the contrary, the public sector kept strictly within its proportion of the national investment programme; too strictly, I sometimes thought. It was the unpredictable and uncontrollable private production and sale that went astray. The retort can justly be made, in the instance given, that the private producer was engaged in the export trade where the conditions are more uncertain and less within the control of the operator. All this is true, but the damage was done before we could catch up with the results: and these were serious and cumulative. The carefully arranged priorities went all wrong. The British roads were thronged with expensive buses, trucks and trailers, all adding to the national cost of transport; and this at a time when more essential forms of consumption were denied the population.

That last sentence brings us up against one of the central issues posed by modern society. What is most essential and who is to decide it?

What are the most worthy objects on which to spend surplus productive capacity? For the sake of simplicity I am accepting the existing pattern of production and consumption, although by no means do I agree with it. After providing for the kind of life we have been leading as a social aggregate, there is an increment left over that we can use as we wish. What would we like to do with it?

Now the first thing to be noticed is that in the competitive society the question is never asked. It is not a public question at all. It cannot be publicly asked with any advantage because it is not capable of a public decision which can be carried out. Therefore in this most vital sphere, the shaping of the kind of future we would like to lead, we are disfranchised at the very outset. We are unable to discuss it because the disposal of the economic surplus is not ours to command. This means, as I have pointed out in previous chapters, that whereas we consider the world of nature capable of being subordinated to our will, society is left uncharted and therefore unpredictable. Where society is to go from here does not lie within the competence of any assembly of statesmen, in any part of the capitalist world, so long as the assumptions of competitive capitalism remain unchallenged. The surplus is merely a figure of speech. Its reality consists in a million and one surpluses in the possession of as many individuals. Political economy is a study of how the surpluses have been disposed of, and consequently of how they are likely to be dealt with in the future. It is not a science of what should happen to them. That belongs to the world of morals.

If we reduce the question to the realm where we have brought it, that is to say, to the individual possessor of the surplus, the economist will provide us with a ready answer. He will tell us that the surplus owner will invest it in the goods for which he thinks there will be a profitable sale. The choice will lie with those able to buy the goods the owner of the surplus will proceed to produce. This means that those who have been most successful for the time being, that is, the money owners, will in the sum of their individual decisions determine the character of the economy of the future. This is an extremely simplified version of what actually happens, but, nevertheless, it is the core of the defence of *laissez-faire* economics.

At first sight this seems a satisfactory answer to our question. In fact it answers both questions; what is most desirable and who decides it? The one who decides is the one who has been most successful. That seems all right. What can be more reasonable than that the successful should shape the future? Would you have the failures decide it? That would be merely sour grapes.

There is a wide range of answers that could be made and indeed have been made to these questions. There is, for example, the argument that many of the successful are only so because they happen to be the children of their parents and have inherited success rather than achieved it. From this it follows that the failures are so because they selected the wrong parents. Then there is the old Socialist argument, always potent, that mere survival is not a test of superior virtues, for in that case, in a swamp, flies would be superior to men. Some possessors of money have got it by sharp practice, others by gambling, yet others by nepotism and still more by social connexions. The list is endless.

But the final answer does not lie in any of these or in all of them combined. The answer consists in the fact that the kind of society which emerges from the sum of individual choices is not one which commends itself to the generality of men and women. It must be borne in mind that the successful were not choosing a type of society. They were only deciding what they thought could be bought and sold most profitably. Nothing was farther from their mind than making a judgement on the kind of society that mankind should live in. That question is no more posed for them than it is for the social group as a whole, in a *laissez-faire* society.

There are many reasons why capitalist society does not command the assent of the masses. There is to begin with the sense of injustice arising from gross inequalities. This is a fertile source of discontent and will always render capitalist society unstable. But I do not consider this by itself as fatal to the existing order. There have been inequalities throughout the history of mankind, but they have not always proved incompatible with a certain degree of social stability. Complete equality is a motive that has never moved large masses for any decisive length of time. It has inspired sects and special orders but it does not appear to be a condition congenial to normal living. There are probably causes deep in the human psyche to explain this, but they lie outside the province of this book. A sense of injustice does not derive solely from the existence of inequality. It arises from the belief that the inequality is capricious, unsanctioned by usage and, most important of all, senseless.

It is commonly said that we are all born unequal, but surely that is the wrong way of expressing it. True we are born of parents who occupy different positions in society; and therefore children start their lives with varying advantages. But that is a difference of social situation and not intrinsic in the children. It would be more correct to say that we are born with different potential aptitudes than that we are born unequal. How these will develop and show themselves will depend upon the kind of social complex we get into. Whether the special aptitudes, qualities or temperament we are born with turn out to be of later advantage, and place us higher in the social scale than others, will turn upon whether they are sufficiently cultivated, and equally important, whether they happen to be of the sort our particular kind of society finds valuable. Different dispositions at the start will result in different social status at the end to the extent that they are favoured by circumstance. In this I am ignoring for the moment the advantages conferred by class and wealth.

The expression that we are born unequal is tendentious because it implies that social rank is biologically decided for us at the outset. Our differences are acted upon by different sorts of social soil. Some flourish while others languish. The fault often lies 'in our stars' and not in us.

I have not found that workers resent higher rewards where they manifestly flow from personal exertion and superior qualities. Thus piecework is universally accepted if its incidence is fair and expresses the result of harder or more skilful work. We all applaud proper recognition for the scientist, the artist and the inventor. Nor indeed is there as yet a disposition to object to the higher incomes awarded certain of the professional classes. But here qualifications are beginning to be heard. It was always accepted that professional social standards should be higher than the general standard because so many unremunerative years had to be spent at school and university to fit the student for future work. The higher income was a compensation for earlier deprivation of income. The situation has changed and continues to change quite markedly. A high percentage of professional students are now educated at the expense of public funds, and during their student years they enjoy a tolerably comfortable standard of life unencumbered by the debts they formerly had to incur. This is bringing about a shift of opinion among those engaged in what are considered the humbler manual occupations. When the funds for training were provided by mortgaging the future, or by great sacrifices on the part of the parents of the student, there was an obvious social sanction for the higher income levels.[14] In present circumstances, there is no disposition to lower professional living standards. That would be a retrograde step and is opposed to the climate of opinion in all classes. But there is a very definite feeling that the gap should be narrowed and that the lower income groups should be allowed to catch up a little.

In the meantime the assumptions that attach themselves to those in the higher income groups are as assertive as ever. It is not unusual to hear members of the professions complain that some piecework miners are able to earn almost as much as themselves. It does not seem to occur to them that their own jobs are more attractive, and what is even more to the point, becoming more accessible than formerly; and that consequently there is no longer the same justification for differential income levels.

Working-class families often skimped and saved to send a bright son or daughter to the university. The student led a frugal life, often doing odd jobs, when these could be got, and working with his family in the holidays. In my own family, my brothers and I went down the pit on leaving elementary school, but our sisters were sent to college. This quite often happened in the mining and steel districts of South Wales. The girls were trained for school teaching largely because there were no jobs open to them in areas given over almost entirely to heavy industry.

In my recollection we did not envy our sisters. On the contrary, we took pride in their scholastic success. In return it often happened that the family budget was helped in later years if professional posts could be found at or near the family home. This was part of the texture of family life among the artisan community. When the bad years came and unemployment cut cruelly into our already limited resources it became more difficult. But even then it was surprising how tenaciously we clung to the hope of superior educational opportunities for those of our family who could benefit by them.

In many respects the situation is different today. Professional careers are more common. Educational authorities and the state have loosened their purse strings to such an extent that the majority of university places are provided by public monies. The family contribution is now the least important factor in meeting the expenses of academic training. What was formerly a private sacrifice is now a public benefaction. The young worker in industry now pays for the academic training of those able to enjoy it. There is nothing wrong in this. Indeed, it could not be otherwise. Some have to work while others learn. But it does cast doubt on the traditional reasons why there is such a gap between the social standards of the professional classes and those of the other occupations whose abstinence from consumption it is that supports the revenues of the universities.

The standard of life of the student is higher than that of the industrial worker who maintains him. He usually lives in more congenial surroundings, and his holidays are more generous than the week or fortnight the industrial worker has only just managed to get inserted into his contract with his employers.

Nevertheless, when the professional worker completes his training his expectations are based on traditional values that are losing their old validity. This is beginning to produce tensions in unexpected directions. Many of the professional classes have retirement pensions and emoluments attached to their professions and these are on a scale commensurate with their salaries. The retirement pensions of the majority of the industrial population are those fixed by national insurance. The disparity is obvious. Many trade unions are moving to remedy this anomaly. But as some industries are more favourably situated in this respect than others, the result is bound to produce a great deal of heart burning.

The situation is not made easier by virtue of the fact that occupational retirement schemes contain early retirement ages, partly because of the old bogy, fear of unemployment, and partly because older retirement age would retard promotion.

This is a special problem in itself. It is too wide a subject to be exhausted here. But it is relevant to call attention to the fact that the conventions that have grown up around the social expectations of salary and wage-earners no longer correspond as much as formerly with the objective facts. There is no quick and easy solution. Too much dislocation would be caused thereby. What can be expected is a shift in opinion, or it will become even more difficult to man up industrial occupations to which outmoded conceptions of status and reward still attach.

Resentment against inequality occurs when it quite clearly flows from social accident, such as inherited wealth or occupations of no superior social value. The mere ownership of property is not a social service in itself. Nor is great wealth possible by personal exertions and qualities alone. It derives from the power to exploit the exertions of others. This is a predatory power made possible by carrying over into modern society the concepts of barbarism, when theft, raid and pillage were accepted ways of acquiring property. It was even tolerable and carried with it a certain justification in the early days of capitalist society when the personal element was still a significant factor in the process of capital accumulation. This is no longer the case except in small businesses.

No one in modern industrial society starts off with nothing. He inherits, as a citizen, a vast plexus of industrial techniques piled up by the whole past of mankind. When, therefore, a so-called self-made man boasts that he started with nothing and carved out a fortune for himself he is talking unmitigated nonsense. If he had had nothing but himself he would have ended up with nothing. What in fact happens is that each of us stands on the shoulders of the past, a past that includes all the great names in history. Such knowledge as we possess is transmitted to us by the medium of a more and more complex social organization. The scientist whose achievements we now set out to exploit would never have made the arrogant assertion that he had started off with nothing. He had himself painfully acquired the accumulated corpus of knowledge in his own particular field and proceeded to add his own contribution, big or little, as the case might be.

It is no answer that a great industrial society like the United States still makes it possible for individuals to amass great fortunes. The fortunes rarely, if ever, correspond to the contribution their owners have made either to the material wealth of the community or to its well-being in other directions. They represent the reward in most cases of concentrated acquisitiveness. Their owners manage to get a favoured position on the banks of the streams of wealth flowing through the community and suck up greedily as much as they can before they are edged out by stronger rivals. The effort they make to get into that position, and to hold it as long as possible, deceives them into thinking they have worked hard and tirelessly for what they get. And so they have, as their duodenal ulcers testify. But if effort alone is enough to justify great wealth, a burglar is on the same basis as a millionaire. What matters is the social utility of the effort, not the effort itself. The subjective consciousness of exertion is no test of its objective merit.

What we are witnessing is the private acquisition of wealth socially produced. And not only is the wealth itself a product of social teamwork, but the ideas that lead to new wealth are now the result of many trained workers acting in concert. It is true that one will get an inspiration that may lead to new agents of production and promising themes for further exploration. But the inspiration will be an evocation induced by co-operative effort. It is possible to list a long series of inventions produced in this way. But it rarely happens that those engaged in experiment and research, and eventually discovery, are the ones who amass huge fortunes. These are usually achieved by a different type of individual altogether. The prototype of the successful man in modern industrial society is not the scientist, the inventor, the scholar. It is the financier, the gambler, and those with social pull. The others share sometimes, it is true, but their share is modest compared with the oligarchs and tycoons; and they don't usually keep their share for long. They are no match for the commercial prowlers.

Thus there is a sense of injustice in modern society and this induces a feeling of instability even in normal circumstances. The rewards are not in keeping with social worth, and the consciousness of this, both among the successful and the unsuccessful, will simmer and bubble, blowing up into geysers of political and social disturbance in times of economic stress.

But as I said earlier, I do not think the existing social order is threatened with destruction from this source alone. The chief causes of instability in capitalist society are unemployment and the fear of it; resentment against preventable poverty; depersonalization of the worker, and, of course, war. With the problem of war I shall deal in a separate chapter.

The belief that poverty is preventable is a natural outcome of the triumphs of the machine age. It is a relatively new mood for mankind. It has been a ferment working in the minds of the masses of Europe ever since the Industrial Revolution emancipated the individual from reliance upon his own muscular power supplemented by his domesticated animals. It has now spread to the Orient. Its consequences will not be exhausted there this century. There is at present a spate of books seeking to prove that the growth of population in the Oriental countries, if it continues, will make it impossible to maintain even the existing standards of consumption. A new Malthusianism is in the air. There are those who prophesy starvation for two-thirds of the human race, and at the same time the West pours torrents of wealth into the creation of a vast war machine. But of that later.

The belief that poverty was the inescapable lot of man served as a social cement throughout most of human history. 'By the sweat of thy brow shalt thou eat thy bread,' uttered as a curse, ended by being a discipline – the most effective discipline of all – more potent than armies and prisons, the frown of authority, the exhortations of the priests. It carried more weight than all these combined just because it was so obviously true. And being true it set a limit to the possibilities of political disturbance and social upheaval. Even today the argument that an equal distribution of existing wealth would not raise the average by an appreciable amount has considerable potency. How much more so was this the case when all there was to divide was infinitesimal compared with the immense wealth of modern society. It kept the poor in subjection because even successful rebellion could not serve to mitigate the rigours of toil by anything much that could be measured. It begot quietism, and even the mortification of the flesh, all the more so when there was not much flesh to mortify.

Against a drab background of universal poverty, the pomp and circumstance of barbarism was the only source of colour and pageantry, ritual, exaltation and a certain elevation of the spirit. A million small contributions went to the building of a cathedral, a mosque, a temple, a pyramid, or a great mansion. But when they had been created they served to enrich many individual lives that would have remained unillumined if the collective effort had not been made.

In time people came to resent the exactions that made such splendour possible. But it is interesting to observe that their resentment grew as they became more able to afford to be resentful. Nor is this difficult to understand. As their individual lives grew more urbane they were less dependent on the mass provision of colour and pageantry. It seems to be a part of normal psychology to resent loss of savings as much as, or more than, loss of earnings. This is probably because the self-denial that went into the savings endear them more.

With the conviction that poverty was no longer inescapable, the 'framework of the past,' to use H. G. Wells's phrase, was broken. Philosophy and religious resignation gave place to rebellion and self-assertion. The floodgates were open. They are still open; and now right throughout the world. 'If some Richelieu does not stem the torrent of private judgement,' cried Madame de Renal to Julien in Stendhal's *Le Rouge et le Noir*, 'all is lost.' The torrent is still flowing, but now private judgement is increasingly aimed at the social barriers erected against the conquest of poverty.

It is possible that in the United States the argument still holds good that private economic adventure offers the best means for the development of industrial techniques; but in Europe the belief no longer holds. The arteries of capitalism in Europe have hardened. The assault on poverty is now recognized more and more as a collective operation with private activities playing a subordinate role. It is one of the ironies of life that insistence on state, collective, or communal action – call it what you will – is fostered by American intervention. With Marshall aid went a demand that it should be used to rejuvenate European industry. It did not seem to occur to the stout supporters of private enterprise in the American Senate that they were asking for the virtual abandonment of uncontrolled private enterprise. They demanded a plan. Now if there is one thing you cannot plan it is competition. Of course you can have competitive planning and that is apparently what Italy, for example, has been doing: with results that can hardly be described as happy.[15]

The fact must be faced that Europe will never return to the practices, conventions and principles of pre-war. There is not only political paralysis in Western Europe; there is a profound lack of confidence in conventional values, and this is true for all social classes. This is accompanied by a deep spiritual malaise arising from a prolonged hesitancy to choose between a number of proffered alternatives. It is probably true that Western Europe would have gone Socialist after the war if Soviet behaviour had not given it too grim a visage. Soviet Communism and Socialism are not yet sufficiently distinguished in many minds.

The large Communist votes in Western Europe, especially in France and Italy, are evidence that millions of men and women do not believe that competitive private enterprise has any future; at least of a sort that would commend itself to them. It is extremely doubtful whether the Communist vote is a vote for Communism. It is partly a protest vote and partly a demand for Democratic

Socialism after the fashion of the first five years of the British Labour government.

It was the promise to abolish preventable poverty that helped people to tolerate all the manifold injustices and shortcomings of capitalist society, just as it was the belief that it could not be abolished that protected the social classes from suicidal collision in previous societies.

With the discovery that capitalism was failing in the very sphere where it was thought to be triumphant, the end of competitive industrialism was merely a question of time. This failure was apparent in Great Britain in the years between the two wars, as I have mentioned briefly in a previous chapter, but an illustration from my own experience may present the point less abstractly.

The constituency I represent in Parliament belongs to the district which was the cradle of heavy industry in Britain. Ebbw Vale, Tredegar, Dowlais, Merthyr Tydfil, Rhymney, all these are names familiar to students of the Industrial Revolution. They possessed most of the requisites for heavy industry; coal, iron ore, limestone. As time went on the iron ore was exhausted and this was held to justify the recession of heavy industry from these parts. The explanation is only partly true. They are only twenty miles from the coast, and as our iron ore had now to come from abroad in the main, a twenty-mile haulage cannot be held to justify uprooting whole townships with all that is involved in such an operation. Some may say this is a parochial view induced by local affiliations and the natural reluctance of a Member of Parliament to witness the migration of his constituents. As the argument develops the reader will see there is more in it than that. A twenty-mile transport problem for the conveyance of only one element in the industrial process should not lead to the destruction of so much social equipment. Nor would this happen if the same authority was responsible for the social as well as the industrial capital. But the social capital was a communal preoccupation, while the industrial capital was a private one. If the social cost of transfer were added to the cost of the new works on the new site, the economics would work out differently. But this is not my immediate concern here.

If the migration of industry had served the purpose of an expanding steel industry, the dislocation of so many people's lives might have been tolerable. But this was not the case. Private initiative in British steel production was exhausting itself. Old out-of-date steel plants were kept ticking over by means of bank overdrafts. London finance was not concerned with preserving the foundations of British industry. That was not its responsibility. But at this point an essay in collective action was tried. Under the direction of Mr Philip Snowden, then Labour Chancellor of the Exchequer, the Bank of England was persuaded to establish a Bankers' Industrial Development Corporation to provide finance mainly for steel undertakings that could not raise money in the open market. The prospect of profit had failed the British steel industry. Other motivations had to take its place.

It is necessary to emphasize that we are here speaking of nothing less than the survival of Great Britain as an industrial power; and that means the survival of her teeming population. Competitive enterprise in Britain had run into a cul-de-sac from which it had to be rescued by state action. But this is only part of the story. Worse is to come.

The corporation found the necessary finance for the reconstruction and re-equipment of a number of steel undertakings that are now flourishing. Unfortunately, Ebbw Vale was not among them. This led me to seek an interview with the Chancellor of the Exchequer, who by then was Mr Neville Chamberlain. He in his turn sent me to the Secretary to the Treasury, who in his turn passed me on to the Secretary to the Development Corporation. At last I was interviewing the official supposed to be engaged in rebuilding the steel industry of Britain both for present and future needs. The conversation was illuminating. He was an extremely able man. What he could do he did very efficiently. But he had to work within the limits of policy laid down for him. When I asked about the prospects of finance to put the Ebbw Vale steel plant back into modern steel production he shook his head. 'Impossible,' he said. That was bad enough. But the reason he gave was worse. It was not, as you might think, that Ebbw Vale was badly sited, and that a new steelworks should go elsewhere. As I have said there was an argument for this, though in my opinion a bad one. No, the reason he gave was that his advisers saw no market prospects for any more steelworks in Great Britain in addition to the ones already in their schemes. Apparently we had reached the maximum steel production for which there seemed any prospect of profitable consumption. What was that? It was somewhere in the region of ten to eleven million tons per annum, much of it from obsolete plants with high production costs.

An industrial economist had just made a calculation that if we in Britain at that time were using steel to the same amount per head of population as the United States we should be consuming nineteen million tons per annum. Yet our steel production was to be stabilized at ten to eleven millions. And this with thousands of steel workers idle, and unlimited tasks left undone for want of steel and its ancillaries.

We have now climbed to between sixteen and seventeen million tons per year, mainly under national direction and control, and there is still a distance to travel if Britain is to play its proper part in the world.

The bleak sequel was that during the war we had to convey precious steel with the loss of still more precious lives across the Atlantic; and Britain's industrial recovery after the war was slower and more expensive in foreign dollar currency than it need have been. There was no justification for the smugly complacent advertisements that have appeared in the British press ever since the war. These were intended to convince the British people that all was well in the world of steel and that whatever else we lacked, these far-sighted, efficient and enterprising steelmasters could be relied upon to serve the needs of the nation in war and peace. Certainly technical knowledge we had in abundance and the men to apply it. But we had failed to realize that in Britain, at least, the propulsions of private economic adventure had lost their force. Excessive caution had taken the place of self-confidence: we had organized scarcity and high profits instead of expanding production and the acceptance of risk.

The same story is true in their different ways of coal and textiles, power stations and oil refining plants.[16] If private enterprise had been left to its own devices the standard of living of the British people would be lower than it is today, and the prospects for the future grim indeed for the population of this island.

We have escaped from the greater poverty that would have been our fate. But not by the automatism of private competition so dear to the heart of some economists. This had demonstrably failed. Public intervention at one point after another alone served to protect us from the industrial lethargy that had overtaken vital areas of our economy.

NOTE 13
It is worth noting that, under the powerful stimulus given to it by the Labour government's fiscal policies, total capital investment now takes a far greater share of the national product than under pre-war Conservative administrations. In 1938 some 15 per cent of the national product was devoted to capital investment. In 1947 the comparable figure was 19 per cent, rising to 22 per cent in 1948. It has been maintained at or above 20 per cent ever since.

NOTE 14
In Britain, even those who pay for their own education are now heavily subsidized indirectly by the financial help to university services from the University Grants Committee..

NOTE 15
The following statistics give some idea of the extent to which the so-called 'free enterprise' countries, whose policies have been much favoured by the British Conservative Party and by powerful American interests, have fallen behind those countries with Democratic Socialist governments.

Industrial Production in 1950
1938 = 100
(European countries contributing more than
1 per cent of Europe's industrial production.)
Sweden   165

Denmark	155
Norway	151
Great Britain	150
Netherlands	139
France	121
Belgium	120
Italy	109
Western Germany	96

Agricultural Production in 1950
1934–8 = 100
(European countries contributing more than
5 per cent of Europe's agricultural production.)

Great Britain	121
Italy	102
France	96
Spain	90
Western Germany	84

The figures have been taken from the *Economic Survey of Europe in 1950*, published by the Economic Commission for Europe.

NOTE 16

Particularly has this been true in the case of the petroleum industry. Realizing in 1946 that Britain's dollar problem would involve indefinite petrol restrictions unless other steps were taken, the Labour government sought to encourage the construction of a series of oil refineries in Britain and gave its approval to a scheme estimated to cost £125 million. In April 1947, work began on selected refinery sites at Stanlow, Shellhaven and Llandarcy.

Six months later Lord Woolton, Chairman of the Conservative Party, was demanding 'in these days of over-full employment there should be a postponement of all works of a public nature, and a discouragement of all capital expenditure, whether by the Government or by private industry.' This demand was hastily supported by many other leading Conservatives and a few tame economists hanging on to their coat-tails.

The Labour government ignored this advice, and pressed on with its plans. In 1948 a further refinery was started at Grangemouth, and in May 1949, a commencement was made on another one at Fawley – a project to which considerable aid was given by the United States administration. By 1952, as a result of these endeavours, helped by government intervention and encouragement, we shall be refining 15,500,000 more tons of oil than in 1939.

D

5

A Free Health Service

THE field in which the claims of individual commercialism come into most immediate conflict with reputable notions of social values is that of health. That is true both for curative and preventive medicine. The preventive health services of modern society fight the battle over a wider front and therefore less dramatically than is the case with personal medicine.

Yet the victories won by preventive medicine are much the most important for mankind. This is so not only because it is obviously preferable to prevent suffering than to alleviate it. Preventive medicine, which is merely another way of saying health by collective action, builds up a system of social habits that constitute an indispensable part of what we mean by civilization. In this sphere values which are in essence Socialist challenge and win victory after victory against the assertions and practice of the competitive society.

Modern communities have been made tolerable by the behaviour patterns imposed upon them by the activities of the sanitary inspector and the medical officer of health. It is true, these rarely work out what they do in terms of Socialist philosophy; but that does not alter the fact that the whole significance of their contribution is its insistence that the claims of the individual shall subordinate themselves to social codes that have the collective well-being for their aim, irrespective of the extent to which this frustrates individual greed.

It is only necessary to visit backward countries, or the backward parts of even the most advanced countries, to see what happens when this insistence is overborne. There, the small well-to-do classes furnish themselves with some of the machinery of good sanitation, such as a piped water supply from their own wells, and modern drainage and cesspools. Having satisfied their own needs, they fight strenuously against finding the money to pay for a good general system that would make the same conveniences available to everyone else.

The more advanced the country, the more its citizens insist on a pure water supply, on laws against careless methods of preparing and handling food, and against the making and advertising of harmful drugs. Powerful vested interests with profits at stake compel the public authorities to fight a sustained battle against the assumption that the pursuit of individual profit is the best way to serve the general good.

The same is true in relation to contagious diseases. These are kept at bay by the constant war society is waging in the form of collective action conducted by men and women who are paid fixed salaries. Neither payment by results nor the profit motive are relevant. It would be a fanatical supporter of the competitive society who asserted that the work done in the field of preventive medicine shows the enslavement of the individual to what has come to be described in the United States as 'statism', and is therefore to be deplored. The more likely retort is that all these are part of the very type of society I am opposing. That is true. But they do not flow from it. They have come in spite of it. They stem from a different order of values. They have established themselves and they are still winning their way by hard struggle. In claiming them, capitalism proudly displays medals won in the battles it has lost.

When we consider the great discoveries in medicine that have revolutionized surgery and the treatment of disease, the same pattern appears. They were made by dedicated men and women whose work was inspired by values that have nothing to do with the rapacious bustle of the stock exchange: Pasteur, Simpson, Jenner, Lister, Semelweiss, Fleming, Domagk, Roentgen – the list is endless. Few of these would have described themselves as Socialists, but they can hardly be considered representative types of the competitive society.

The same story is now being unfolded in the field of curative medicine. Here individual and collective action are joined in a series of dramatic battles. The collective principle asserts that the resources of medical skill and the apparatus of healing shall be placed at the disposal of the patient, without charge, when he or she needs them; that medical treatment and care should be a communal responsibility

that they should be made available to rich and poor alike in accordance with medical need and by no other criteria. It claims that
financial anxiety in time of sickness is a serious hindrance to
recovery, apart from its unnecessary cruelty. It insists that no society
can legitimately call itself civilized if a sick person is denied medical
aid because of lack of means.

Preventable pain is a blot on any society. Much sickness and often
permanent disability arise from failure to take early action, and this
in its turn is due to high costs and the fear of the effects of heavy bills
on the family. The records show that it is the mother in the average
family who suffers most from the absence of a free health service.
In trying to balance her domestic budget she puts her own needs
last.

Society becomes more wholesome, more serene, and spiritually
healthier, if it knows that its citizens have at the back of their consciousness the knowledge that not only themselves, but all their
fellows, have access, when ill, to the best that medical skill can
provide. But private charity and endowment, although inescapably
essential at one time, cannot meet the cost of all this. If the job is to
be done, the state must accept financial responsibility.

When I was engaged in formulating the main principles of the
British Health Service, I had to give careful study to various proposals for financing it, and as this aspect of the scheme is a matter of
anxious discussion in many other parts of the world, it may be useful
if I set down the main considerations that guided my choice. In the
first place, what was to be its financial relationship with national
insurance; should the health service be on an insurance basis? I
decided against this. It had always seemed to me that a personal
contributory basis was peculiarly inappropriate to a national health
service. There is, for example, the question of the qualifying period.
That is to say, so many contributions for this benefit, and so many
more for additional benefits, until enough contributions are eventually paid to qualify the contributor for the full range of benefits.

In the case of health treatment this would give rise to endless
anomalies, quite apart from the administrative jungle which would
be created. This is already the case in countries where people insure
privately for operations as distinct from hospital or vice versa.

Whatever may be said for it in private insurance, it would be out of place in a national scheme. Imagine a patient lying in hospital after an operation and ruefully reflecting that if the operation had been delayed another month he would have qualified for the operation benefit. Limited benefits for limited contributions ignore the overriding consideration that the full range of health machinery must be there in any case, independent of the patient's right of free access to it.

Where a patient claimed he could not afford treatment, an investigation would have to be made into his means, with all the personal humiliation and vexation involved. This scarcely provides the relaxed mental condition needed for a quick and full recovery. Of course there is always the right to refuse treatment to a person who cannot afford it. You can always 'pass by on the other side'. That may be sound economics. It could not be worse morals.

Some American friends tried hard to persuade me that one way out of the alleged dilemma of providing free health treatment for people able to afford to pay for it would be to fix an income limit below which treatment would be free while those above must pay. This makes the worst of all worlds. It still involves proof, with disadvantages I have already described. In addition it is exposed to lying and cheating and all sorts of insidious nepotism.

And these are the least of its shortcomings. The really objectionable feature is the creation of a two-standard health service, one below and one above the salt. It is merely the old British Poor Law system over again. Even if the service given is the same in both categories there will always be the suspicion in the mind of the patient that it is not so, and this again is not a healthy mental state.

The essence of a satisfactory health service is that the rich and the poor are treated alike, that poverty is not a disability, and wealth is not advantaged.

Two ways of trying to meet the high cost of sickness are the group insurance and the attachment of medical benefits to the terms of employment. Group insurance is merely another way of bringing the advantages of collective action to the service of the individual. All the insurance company does is to assess the degree of risk in any particular field, work out the premium required from a given number of individuals to cover it, add administrative cost and dividends, and then sell the result to the public. They are purveyors of the law of averages. They convert economic continuity, which is a by-product of communal life, into a commodity, and it is then bought and sold like any other commodity.

What is really bought and sold is the group, for the elaborate actuarial tables worked out by the insurance company are nothing more than a description of the patterns of behaviour of that collectivity which is the subject of assessment for the time being. To this the company adds nothing but its own profits. This profit is therefore wholly gratuitous because it does not derive from the creation of anything. Group insurance is the most expensive, the least scientific, and the clumsiest way of mobilizing collective security for the individual good.

In many countries the law implicitly recognizes this because the insurance company is required to invest some, if not all, of its income in trustee stock, national bonds and debentures. In other words, the company must invest in those properties which bear the strongest imprint of continuous communal action. The nearer the investment approaches to those forms of property which are most characteristic of competitive capitalism, the less the element of collective security, and therefore the less desirable from the point of view of insurance. There never can be a clearer case of the private exploitation of a product publicly produced.

Where medical benefits are attached to employment as a term of the contract the situation is somewhat different. Here is an instance where the workers, as occupational groups, succeed in accomplishing what they have failed to do or not tried to do as enfranchised citizens. It has the one advantage that the employer in such a case will be less eager to lobby against legislation for a national health scheme. He may be inclined to support national proposals because these will make others share part of his burden. As a political tactic, therefore, occupational medical benefits have something to be said for them; and the workers enjoy some protection in the meantime while the national scheme is being held up.

But they are no substitute for a national scheme. An industrial basis is too narrow for the wide range of medical needs which should be met, both for the worker and for his family. The incidence of sickness varies from industry to industry and so do the rates of economic obsolescence and unemployment. We had experience of this in Britain where certain of the Approved Societies under the old National Health Insurance recruited a disproportionate number of members from industries with a high degree of sickness and accident rate and affected by serious industrial depression. The result was that these Approved Societies were compelled to curtail benefits to their members, while other societies with a different industrial composition were able to distribute the full benefits. That situation consequently helped the strong and hurt the weak.

There are two final objections to the methods I have been describing. They create a chaos of little or big projects, all aiming at the same end: assisting the individual in time of sickness. A whole network of strong points emerge, each with a vested interest in preventing a rational national scheme from being created. Thus to the property lobby is added the lobby of those who stand to lose under the national project. In the end they may have to be bought out at great cost in time, effort and money.

The second objection is even more serious. These schemes all have for their aim the consumption of the apparatus of health. But they leave the creation of that apparatus without plan and central direction. In place of a rational relationship between all its parts, there arises a patch-quilt of local paternalisms. My experience has taught me that there is no worse enemy to the intelligent planning of a national health service, especially on the hospital side. Warm gushes of self-indulgent emotion are an unreliable source of driving power in the field of health organization. The benefactor tends also to become a petty tyrant, not only willing his cash, but sending his instructions along with it.

The other alternative is a flat rate compulsory contribution for all, covering the full range of health treatment, or a limited part of it. There is no advantage whatever in this. It is merely a form of poll tax with all its disagreeable features. It collects the same from the rich and the poor, and this is manifestly unjust. On no showing can it be called insurance.

One thing the community cannot do is insure against itself. What

it can and must do is to set aside an agreed proportion of the
national revenues for the creation and maintenance of the service it
has pledged itself to provide. This is not so much insurance as a
prudent policy of capital investment. There is a further objection to
a universal contribution, and that is its wholly unnecessary administrative cost – unless it is proposed to have graduated contributions for graduated benefits, and I have already pointed out the
objections to that. Why should *all* have contribution cards if *all* are
assumed to be insured? This merely leads to a colossal record
office, employing scores of thousands of clerks solemnly restating
in the most expensive manner what the law will already have said;
namely, that *all* citizens are in the scheme.

The means of collecting the revenues for the health service are
already in the possession of most modern states, and that is the
normal system of taxation.

This was the course which commended itself to me and it is the
basis of the finance of the British Health Service. Its revenues are
provided by the Exchequer in the same way as other forms of public
expenditure. I am afraid this is not yet fully understood. Many
people still think they pay for the National Health Service by way of
their contribution to the National Insurance Scheme. The confusion
arose because the new service sounded so much like the old National
Health Insurance, and it was launched on the same date as the
National Insurance Scheme. Some part of the misunderstanding was
caused by the propaganda of the British Medical Association,which
warned the people at one time that, although they would be paying
their contributions, the Health Service would not be there to meet
their needs. There was a certain irony about this, because when the
time came for enrolment in the Health Service more than ninety
per cent of the population hastened to get their names in, some
under the impression, helped by the B.M.A. itself, that they had
started paying for it. This gave me some quiet satisfaction.

One of the consequences of the universality of the British Health
Service is the free treatment of foreign visitors. This has given rise
to a great deal of criticism, most of it ill-informed and some of it
deliberately mischievous. Why should people come to Britain and
enjoy the benefits of the free Health Service when they do not

subscribe to the national revenues? So the argument goes. No doubt a little of this objection is still based on the confusion about contributions to which I have referred. The fact is, of course, that visitors to Britain subscribe to the national revenues as soon as they start consuming certain commodities, drink and tobacco for example, and entertainment. They make no direct contribution to the cost of the Health Service any more than does a British citizen.

However, there are a number of more potent reasons why it would be unwise as well as mean to withhold the free service from the visitor to Britain. How do we distinguish a visitor from anybody else? Are British citizens to carry means of identification everywhere to prove that they are not visitors? For if the sheep are to be separated from the goats both must be classified. What began as an attempt to keep the Health Service for ourselves would end by being a nuisance to everybody. Happily, this is one of those occasions when generosity and convenience march together.

The cost of looking after the visitor who falls ill cannot amount to more than a negligible fraction of £399,000,000, the total cost of the Health Service. It is not difficult to arrive at an approximate estimate. All we have to do is look up the number of visitors to Great Britain during one year and assume they would make the same use of the Health Service as a similar number of Britishers. Divide the total cost of the Service by the population and you get the answer. I had the estimate taken out and it amounted to about £200,000 a year.

Obviously this is an overestimate because people who go for holidays are not likely to need a doctor's attention as much as others. However, there it is for what it is worth and you will see it does not justify the fuss that has been made about it.

The whole agitation has a nasty taste. Instead of rejoicing at the opportunity to practice a civilized principle, Conservatives have tried to exploit the most disreputable emotions in this among many other attempts to discredit socialized medicine.

Naturally when Britons go abroad they are incensed because they are not similarly treated if they need the attention of a doctor. But that also I am convinced will come when other nations follow our example and have health services of their own. When that happens

D *

we shall be able to work out schemes of reciprocity, and yet one
more amenity will have been added to social intercourse. In the
meantime let us keep in mind that, here, example is better than
precept.

The National Health Service and the Welfare State have come
to be used as interchangeable terms, and in the mouths of some
people as terms of reproach. Why this is so it is not difficult to
understand, if you view everything from the angle of a strictly
individualistic competitive society. A free health service is pure
Socialism and as such it is opposed to the hedonism of capitalist
society. To call it something for nothing is absurd because everything has to be paid for in some way or another.

But it does mean that the Service is there to be used at the time
you need it without payment anxieties. To put it another way, you
provide, when you are well, a service that will be available if and
when you fall ill. It is therefore an act of collective goodwill and
public enterprise and not a commodity privately bought and sold.
It takes away a whole segment of private enterprise and transfers it
to the field of public administration, where it joins company with
the preventive services and the rest of the communal agencies, by
means of which the new society is being gradually articulated. Nor
should we underestimate the size of the invasion we are making. In
Britain there are more than 340,000 workers of various kinds engaged in the National Health Service. It costs about eight pounds
per head of the population.[17] But a large proportion of this sum
was being paid on private account before the Service started. It is
impossible to estimate the exact amount. Some experts in this field
go so far as to say they doubt whether there is any real net additional
social cost, because of the innumerable harpies who battened on the
sick and who are slowly being eliminated. Be that as it may, there is
no doubting the magnitude of the enterprise. What is surprising is
the smoothness of the transfer and the way it is settling down.

The prophets of disaster have been proved false, as they so often
are when new and ambitious ventures are projected.

And now comes the question so frequently asked: do not all these
free facilities invite abuse? Whenever I was asked that question I
always answered: 'A prerequisite to a study of human behaviour is

that human beings should first be allowed to behave.' When the Service started and the demands for spectacles, dental attention and drugs rocketed upwards the pessimists said: 'We told you so. The people cannot be trusted to use the Service prudently or intelligently. It is bad now but there is worse to come. Abuse will crowd on abuse until the whole scheme collapses.'

Those first few years of the Service were anxious years for those of us who had the central responsibility. We were anxious, not because we feared the principles of the Service were unsound, but in case they would not be given time to justify themselves. Faith as well as works is essential in the early years of a new enterprise.

The question uppermost in my mind at that time was whether a consistent pattern of behaviour would reveal itself among the millions using the Service, and how long would it take for this to emerge? Unless this happened fairly soon it would not be possible to put in reliable estimates for the Budget. The first few estimates for the Health Service seemed to justify the critics. Expenditure exceeded the estimates by large amounts, and Mr Churchill with his usual lack of restraint plunged into the attack. In this he showed less insight than his colleagues, who watched his antics with increasing alarm. They knew the Service was already popular with the people. If the Service could be killed they wouldn't mind, but they would wish it done more stealthily and in such a fashion that they would not appear to have the responsibility.

Ordinary men and women were aware of what was happening. They knew from their own experience that a considerable proportion of the initial expenditure, especially on dentistry and spectacles, was the result of past neglect. When the first rush was over the demand would even out. And so it proved. Indeed, it was proved even beyond the expectations of those of us who had most faith in the Service.

It is not generally appreciated that after only one full year's experience of the Service I was able to put in an estimate which was firm and accurate. This was remarkable. It meant that in so short a space of time we were able to predict the pattern of behaviour of all the many millions of people who would be using the Service in a particular year. Whatever abuses there were, they were not on the

increase. From that point on, any increased expenditure on the
Service would come from its planned expansion and not from unpredictable use and abuse. We now knew the extent to which the
people would use the existing facilities and what it would cost us.
The ground was now firm under our feet. Such abuses as there were
could be dealt with by progressive administrative pressure.[18]

Danger of abuse in the Health Service is always at the point where
private commercialism impinges on the Service; where, for example,
the optician is paid for the spectacles he himself prescribes, or the
dentist gives an unnecessary filling for which he is paid. Abuse
occurs where an attempt is made to marry the incompatible principles of private acquisitiveness with a public service. Does it therefore follow that the solution is to abandon the field to commercialism? Of course not. The solution is to decrease the dependence on
private enterprise. The optical service is a case in point.

I have been told by ophthalmic surgeons that opticians prescribe
spectacles sometimes when they are not really necessary. This, of
course, the opticians hotly resent. The opticians protests would
carry more weight if they were not also purveyors of spectacles.
They thus make a profit out of their own advice and this tends to
cast doubt on the advice itself.

This is an obvious defect in the British Health Service as it is
now. I never intended it to remain. The present arrangements have
always been regarded as temporary, to be replaced as follows. If the
family doctor believes there may be something wrong with your
eyes the best person to advise is the ophthalmic surgeon and not the
ophthalmic optician. The latter is primarily concerned with those
physical abnormalities that lead to defects of vision. The surgeon is
interested in the physiological as well as the anatomical aspects.
Under the revised scheme the patient would be sent to the surgeon,
who would use the optician to give a reading of the eyes and so save
his own time. Spectacles would then be provided only if the surgeon
thought them necessary.

Ophthalmic surgeons tell me that if this scheme were in operation
fewer spectacles would be in use. And it would be to the advantage
of the patient to be examined by the surgeon in the first instance, for
he might find in the eyes evidence of morbidity of wider significance,

and thus assist the patient to whatever other treatment might be necessary.

There are other and better ways of dealing with alleged abuses than by throwing in the sponge.

A free Health Service is a triumphant example of the superiority of collective action and public initiative applied to a segment of society where commercial principles are seen at their worst.

'The old system pays me better, so don't interfere.' Who would dare to put it so crudely? But it is as well to keep in mind that a public undertaking of this magnitude is big business. It touches trade and industry at a hundred sensitive points. A striking illustration of this was provided by our efforts to take proper care of the deaf. It had always seemed to me that this affliction had received too little attention. Deafness is a grievous handicap, worse some say even than blindness, though here we must speak with diffidence, because no one who has not suffered both can really judge. But this at least is agreed: deafness causes much personal suffering and industrial loss. The mechanical aids to deafness were often deficient, and always too expensive for all but a tiny section of those in need.

The way that seemed to offer the best chance of success was to bring the hearing specialist and the aural technicians into conference with each other, to see if a satisfactory aid could be devised, which could then be put into mass production and distributed through the hospitals. The effort met with outstanding success. By September 1951, one hundred and fifty-two thousand aids had been distributed and the users are enthusiastic about them.[19] They cost approximately one tenth of those on sale commercially. There is no reason why, after the home demand has been met, they should not prove the basis of a thriving export trade.

By bulk ordering of common essentials and cutting out unnecessary retail profit margins, as in the instance given, substantial economies can be made.

It is significant that few Conservatives mention this side of the Health Service. They are silent where economics could be made at the expense of profits. The possibilities of bulk ordering of whole ranges of hospital equipment and necessities, such as blankets and linen, were realized early in the development of the scheme. In order to extend the advantages of this over a wider field of public expenditure the Supply Department of the Ministry of Health was made responsible for the medical needs of the Armed Forces. When all these are fully integrated, the result should make a significant impact on the private sector of the industries affected. The manufacturers will be afforded a reliable estimate of the requirements of the public authorities and can adjust their production flows accordingly, while improved specifications should improve quality and reduce cost.

But the hardest task for any public representative charged with the duty of making a free Health Service available to the community is overcoming the fears, real and imaginary, of the medical profession. His task is to reconcile the general public interest with their sectional claims. No pressure groups are more highly organized in Britain than the professions, and among these the medical professions are the strongest.

I was anxious to ensure that the general practitioner should be able to earn a reasonable living without having to aim at a register which would be too large to admit of good doctoring. To accomplish this I suggested a graduated system of capitation payments which would be highest in the medium ranges and lower in the higher. This would have discouraged big lists by lessening the financial inducement. The B.M.A. refused this, although now I am told they are ready to reopen the question. Had they agreed at the time the position of doctors in the overdoctored areas of the country would have been made easier as redistribution over the country as a whole gradually took place.

I have a warm spot for the general practitioner despite his tempestuousness. There is a sound case for providing a little more money to help the doctor with a medium list who wants to make a decent living and yet be a good doctor. The injection of several million pounds here would refresh the Service at its most vulnerable point: that is, the family doctor relationship. The family doctor is in many ways the most important person in the Service. He comes into the most immediate and continuous touch with the members of the community. He is also the gateway to all the other branches of the Service. If more is required than he can provide, it is he who puts the patient in touch with the specialist services.[20]

He is also the most highly individualistic member of the medical world. As soon as he leaves medicine he seems to think in slogans. These are shot through with political animus of the most violent description – usually Conservative. I speak here primarily of the British Medical Association. The Medical Practitioners' Union on the other hand is a progressive body, affiliated to the Trades Union Congress and more up-to-date in its views. But it was with the B.M.A. I had to negotiate. I usually met its representatives when they had come hot from a conference at which the wildest speeches had been made, frequently by the very men who then had to try to come to terms with the people they had been so immoderately denouncing.

I enjoyed the challenge. My trade union experience had taught me to distinguish between the atmosphere of the mass demonstration and the quite different mood of the negotiating table. I was therefore able to discount a great deal of what had been said from the rostrum. Also it was easy for me to enable them to win victories, for they had usually worked themselves up into a fever of protest against proposals which had never been made. Thus they would 'never be made into civil servants'.[21] As I never intended they should, I was able to concede the point without difficulty.

Then there must be 'free choice of doctor'. I myself was most anxious to insist on this, for I saw in it one of the most important safeguards for the public. The right of the patient to leave his doctor and choose another whenever he liked had a double edge that the B.M.A. spokesmen did not fully appreciate until later. Then there was the demand for full rights of free expression of opinion, both about the Health Service and anything else. To this again I was most ready to respond, as it had never occurred to me that anything otherwise had been intended.

And so it went on from one blown-out slogan to another. Indeed, I warned the leaders of the profession that they were making a fundamental mistake in strategy. They were mobilizing their forces to fight a battle that was never likely to begin. When later I was able to make a considered statement in Parliament giving a solemn undertaking to abide by principles that were my own from the very start, the B.M.A. found its forces leaving the field just when the crucial stage in the struggle was reached.

In speaking of the medical profession, I must not be thought to be speaking at the same time of the individual men and women who make it up. In their case, as in so many others, the psychology of the profession as a whole is not the sum of its individual parts. Indeed, this seems to be much more the case with doctors than with other social groups. In my dealings with them I was soon made aware of two curious streams of thought. In the first place the general public has no great faith in the medical profession considered as a collectivity, which in no way interferes with a warm attachment between individual doctors and patients. Statesmen anxious to establish a free Health Service should keep that in mind. In a conflict between the profession and the general public the latter will always win if they are courageously led. The pretensions of the medical profession as a special social group are resented by the generality of citizens. They savour too much of caste and privilege. The practice of medicine is still so much more an art than a science that its practitioners do not seem to the laity to be justified in the atmosphere with which they are apt to surround themselves. There is a good deal of hit and miss about general medicine. It is a profession where exact measurement is not easy and the absence of it opens the mind to endless conjecture as to the efficacy of this or that form of treatment.

The doctors themselves insist on this element of unpredictability in the response of individual patients to various forms of treatment. They affirm that individuals differ so much that there is always a high subjective content in the practice of medicine. This arises in a variety of ways; in the medical history of the patient, his work, his relations with his family and with the society of which he is a member. All these apparently have to be taken into account in diagnosis and treatment. This we accept, and indeed it is fairly obvious. What is not so obvious is that the average doctor is equipped by his general education and by temperament to make an assessment of so many imponderables. He requires for this delicate task imaginative sympathy, sensitivity, and a liberal education; and these are not so widespread in the profession as many of us would like to see. That there are such gifted persons we know, and they are

of infinite benefit to suffering mankind. But in this field, with its
margin of error, the quack, the charlatan and the ill-equipped also
flourish, and there are few tests the layman can apply to safeguard
himself.

In my discussions with many of the best members of the medical
professions in Britain they have individually always been ready to
admit this with true scientific humility. But the margin of possible
error which is part of their daily experience does not free them from
what can only be described as a collective arrogance. This is accompanied by waves of something approaching mass hysteria whenever
proposals affecting their profession are advanced. We saw it in
Britain, we have seen it in Australia and New Zealand, and now it
appears to have the medical profession of the United States in its
grip.

In dealing with the medical profession it is wise to make a distinction between three main causes of opposition to the establishment of a free National Health Service. There is the opposition
which springs from political opinion as such. This is part of the
general opposition of Conservative ideas, and it is strong in the
medical profession, though the expression of it tends to be super-
charged with the emotions borrowed from other fears and ambitions.
Second, there is the defence of professional status and material
reward. The latter, of course, they share with other pressure groups.
Then, thirdly, there is the opposition which springs from the fear
that lay interference might affect academic freedom and come
between the doctor and his patient. The third group is the most
legitimate and will unite all the members of the medical world,
from the self-seeking to the truly idealistic. Any health service
which hopes to win the consent of the doctors must allay these fears.
The fear of state interference in academic matters is very strong in
the Western world, although it tends to ignore the power that
patronage already has to influence the pattern of medical investigation. Nevertheless, entitlement to advancement on grounds of merit
alone, free from any tinge of political nepotism, must be jealously
guarded by any self-respecting profession. Nor should less informed
opinion be allowed to influence the medical curriculum. Here there
is no substitute for the refreshment of renovating influences within

the profession itself. Freedom of discussion and a readiness to add to, and receive from, the corpus of accepted knowledge, are the only ways we have yet discovered to safeguard what we have gained, and to open ways to new discoveries.[22] The medical profession is cautious, some say unduly so, in accepting new ideas. This has been impressed upon me over and over again by those who claim to have discovered methods of treatment and cure other than those normally practised by the profession. On the other hand, it is my experience that unorthodox practitioners are often the worst quacks, and when offered a fair hearing, unwilling to expose themselves to the disciplines of controlled experiment and verification. As a general rule they advance testimony in place of evidence and credibility in place of informed conviction.

There is no alternative to self-government by the medical profession in all matters affecting the content of its academic life, although there is every justification for lay co-operation in the economy in which that is carried out. The distinction between the two is real. It is for the community to provide the apparatus of medicine for the doctor. It is for him to use it freely in accordance with the standards of his profession and the requirements of his oath.

This is also the case with respect to the relations between the doctor and his patient. A great deal of nonsense has been talked about this. There never has been any danger that socialized medicine would destroy the privacy of doctor-patient relationship. Such a danger would indeed rupture a health service from the start. The privacy rightly accorded a patient under a health service is much more than is often the case in, for example, private insurance. The consulting room is inviolable and no sensible person would have it otherwise.

The defects in the Health Service that have been brought to light by practical experience lie in quite other directions. Although it is essential to retain parliamentary accountability for the Service, the appointment of members of the various administrative bodies should not involve the Minister of Health. No danger of nepotism arises, as no salaries are attached to the appointments, but election is a better principle than selection. No Minister can feel satisfied that he is making the right selection over so wide a field. The difficulty of applying the principle of election, rather than selection, arises from the fact that no electoral constituency corresponds with the functional requirements of the Service. This is particularly so in the case of hospital organization. Hospitals are grouped in such a way that most, if not all, the different medical specialties are to be found within a given area.

A solution might be found if the reorganization of local government is sufficiently fundamental to allow the administration of the hospitals to be entrusted to the revised units of local government. But no local finances should be levied, for this would once more give rise to frontier problems, and the essential unity of the Service would be destroyed.[23]

Another defect of the Service, which was seen from the beginning, is the existence of pay beds in hospitals. The reason why this was tolerated at all was because it was put to me by the representatives of the royal colleges that in the absence of pay-bed sections in the hospitals the specialists would resort in greater measure to nursing homes. As the full range of medical facilities are available only in the hospitals as a general rule, the specialists should be there, on the spot, as much as possible. The argument is sound, but there can be no doubt that the privilege has been abused. Pay beds are a profitable source of income to the specialists, and there is therefore a disposition to prefer patients who can afford them at the expense of others on the hospital waiting lists. The number of pay beds should be reduced until in course of time they are abolished, unless the abuse of them can be better controlled. The number of 'amenity beds' should be increased. These are beds for which the patient pays a small sum for privacy alone, all the other services being free. These changes would mean a loss of revenue to the National Health Service, but they would cut out a commercial practice which undermines the principle of equality of treatment that is fundamental to the whole conception of the scheme.

Doubtless other defects can be found and further improvements made. What emerges, however, in the final count, is the massive contribution the British Health Service makes to the equipment of a civilized society. It has now become a part of the texture of our national life. No political party would survive that tried to destroy it.

Since this chapter was written, new legislation on the National Health Service has been announced. It confirms our worst fears. If they are carried out the proposals will mutilate the Service in many of its most important activities. There is, however, ample evidence that the British people are reacting sharply against them. This sustains my contention that no government that attempts to destroy the Health Service can hope to command the support of the British people. The great argument about priorities is joined and from it a free Health Service is bound to emerge triumphant.

NOTE 17

In estimating the cost of the Service it is necessary to consider the range of its operations and the facilities it provides. It covers all forms of treatment, mental as well as physical. For the first time these are integrated. Mental ill health is no longer regarded as belonging to a world of its own. I consider this to be one of the outstanding features of the British Health Service. The separation of mental from physical treatment is a survival from primitive conceptions and is a source of endless cruelty and neglect. The mentally ill are looked upon as people who have stepped outside normal intercourse and this fact itself often accentuates and perpetuates the trouble. If at the early stages of mental disturbance the patient is able to get advice, not at a mental institution, but by a mental specialist in a general hospital, then subsequent degeneration can frequently be prevented. The very fact that they go amongst the general streams of patients for consultation and are not hived off on their own is itself a source of helpful self-confidence.

Then there is the provision that enables mental patients to enter mental homes voluntarily and leave when they like. In 1931 voluntary admission represented only 7 per cent of the total admissions, whereas by 1949 the proportion had risen to 63 per cent.

Year	No. of Voluntary Admissions	Proportion of Total Adm ssions %
1931	1,495	7
1932	2,295	10
1933	2,961	13
1934	4,078	17
1935	5,834	24
1936	6,904	27
1937	8,414	31
1938	9,651	35
1939	10,177	36
1940	8,107	32
1941	8,415	35
1942	9,359	38
1943	11,364	43
1944	12,491	45
1945	13,910	47
1946	18,059	51
1947	21,357	54
1948	27,015	59
1949	32,345	63

NOTE 18

Drugs are consumed in too large quantities. Few doctors would disagree with that statement. It was so before the Health Service. Indeed, excessive consumption can be described as one of the diseases of modern civilization. The solution is firmness by the doctor and education of the patient. If there is abuse in this side of the Service the fault lies primarily with the doctor. The chemist cannot dispense what the doctor does not prescribe. Some doctors argue that if they do not give the patient something to take he will leave them and go to another doctor. This is one of the instances of 'free choice of doctor' which, according to the campaign by the B.M.A. when the Service was being formed, was not supposed to exist.

A great deal can be done by a more intensive education of the general population. This would improve the health of the population as well as reduce the burden on the Health Service. Much more imaginative use could be made of the B.B.C. and of television to acquaint the people with the consequences of too much drug-taking. It would also have an appreciable effect on the number of patients attending at the doctors' surgeries.

Already steps had been taken when I was at the Ministry of Health to attack the problem from another and even more promising angle. That was to forbid the consumption in the Service of drugs which are generally advertised. These are usually more expensive and often no better, indeed frequently inferior, to the drugs contained on the official lists and the recognized *Formulary*. The effect of this is threefold. It reduces the pressure of the credulous patient on the doctor when the former demands something he has seen advertised for its miraculous properties. Second, it discourages the production and advertising of these concoctions. Thirdly, it will substantially reduce the cost of prescriptions with the Health Service. These are the answers to whatever abuses may exist on the pharmaceutical side of the British Health Service.

NOTE 19

Number of Hearing Aids – cumulative figures:

	New Patients
Up to December, 1948	7,511
,, ,, ,, 1949	48,734
,, ,, ,, 1950	114,835
,, ,, September, 1951	152,000

NOTE 20

As time goes on it is hoped that general practitioners will find it better to work in groups, whether at a health centre or otherwise. There are advantages in this. The work could be shared between them so as to reduce the strain on the individual doctor. Night calls are an obvious example. Group consultation would put the knowledge and experience of all at the disposal of each, and the natural desire to stand well in the eyes of his fellow craftsmen would tend to raise and maintain standards.

There is still a question-mark against health centres. There is no doubt about their desirability. But there should be a limit to what should be attempted in them. It would be an expensive duplication if they developed into rivals of the out-patient departments of general hospitals. Here further experience is necessary before final decisions are made.

NOTE 21

The fear that the Health Service would result in an army of civil servants was got over by establishing a contractual relationship, not with the Minister of Health but with the boards of governors of teaching hospitals, the regional hospital boards and, in the case of the family doctors, chemists and opticians, with the local executive councils. Thus central responsibility for a national service is reconciled with the principle of dispersed supervision. This is exercised through the medium of voluntary workers. It is not sufficiently understood that all the members of the boards, management committees of hospitals, and members of executive councils serve voluntarily. This is partly responsible for the low administrative cost of the Service.

The separate expenses of the bodies engaged in the administration of the British National Health Service amount to about 3 per cent of the total sum spent. 60 per cent of the expenditure of the hospitals lies outside the jurisdiction of the hospital authorities. Wages and salaries are fixed by national agreement by means of Whitley awards. The area of expenditure left to the hospital authorities within which they can exercise direct economy is, therefore, about 40 per cent of the total.

The local executive councils are composed of representatives of the county councils and county boroughs, committees of the three professions, medical, chemical and optical, along with persons appointed direct by the Minister of Health. This body is responsible for the administration and discipline of the three services. It is therefore the strongest line of defence against abuse, and the body in most immediate contact with members of the general public. On the whole it is working well, except that the county area tends to be too far from the individual citizen. But that must wait upon a reorganization of local government.

NOTE 22

It is one of the distinct advantages of a national service that the use of improved health techniques and new discoveries of treatment are immediately generalized throughout the service. This is an advance on the past where superior methods worked their way slowly down from the few institutions and individuals that could afford them until long afterwards they reached – if they ever did – the poorer members of the community.

The question may be asked, what facilities are made available for research in this set-up ? There is first the Medical Research Council, a body which has been in existence for many years and is under the supervision of a committee of the Privy Council. Some contend that the Medical Research Council should be brought within the administration of the Health Service. I am inclined to support this view. British science has always suffered from the distance which separates 'pure' from applied science. It is this which is partly responsible for the curious phenomenon, referred to on many occasions, that in Britain original discoveries are made which are not followed up in the practical field. Antibiotics is an example.

A closer relationship should be established between the potential user of the results of research and the research itself. The practical and the theoretical are two aspects of the same activity. Their separation is a hangover from the days of cloistered learning.

Research goes on in many of our hospitals all the time, as well as in the private laboratories of commercial companies. More money is now available than at any time in the history of medicine. Most of the teaching hospitals have large sums at their disposal for this purpose. Their endowments were not touched when they were taken over into the Health Service.

But it is not only necessary to discover new knowledge and improve on old techniques. We must also see to it that useful aptitude and skills are not lost. Every war produces its tragic host of maimed, crippled and paralysed. Each time a pool of exceptional knowledge is accumulated to cope with the problem. As the number of patients declines with the passage of time, this contracts, is in danger of being lost and further improvements not pursued with the same drive. The department of the Ministry of Pensions which provides artificial limbs, eyes, ingenious chairs and cars, expanded at the end of the war and would have contracted after the normal pattern. But the civilian population also has its casualties, in the total sometimes as great as those in the services. Here the National Health Service performs an invaluable service. It maintains the pool of skill accumulated by the war and places it at the disposal of the civilian population. The technicians are not dispersed but are kept in continuous employment. If war comes again they will be there, ready immediately to mitigate disability and suffering to the limits of human ingenuity.

When the National Health Service started and free artificial limbs were made available, it was a revelation to witness the condition of the old ones left behind. It was a grim reminder of the extent to which the crippled poor had been neglected.

Number of artificial limbs and surgical appliances, issued from July 1948 to 31 August, 1951:

New Boots	112,556
Leg Instruments	69,987
Trusses	61,852
Belts	388,172
Wigs	28,617
Spinal Supports	80,652
Artificial Legs	30,002
Artificial Arms	6,003
Motor Propelled Tricycles	4,718
Hand Propelled Tricycles	3,190
Other Types of Chairs	11,290

NOTE 23

Local authorities are notoriously unwilling to delegate any of their functions or responsibilities to others. If hospital administration is entrusted to them they must be prepared to give generous support to the staff committees already established in the hospitals. The problem of how to associate the workers in the making of policy and in affairs of day-to-day administration is as real in the hospital world as it is elsewhere.

By revised units of local government is not meant regional local government areas. These would not be local government units in any proper sense of the term.

6

The Transition to Socialism

IT is a dangerous period in the lifetime of a nation when the convictions, beliefs, and values of one epoch are seen to be losing their vitality, and those of the new have not yet won universal acceptance. Many believe they are witnessing the decline of human society, when all that is happening is a change from one type of society to another. Those whose habits and possessions are bound up with the vanishing social order are filled with pessimism. A future which threatens with destruction all that they had come to regard as fixed and eternal, that sacrilegiously laughs at assumptions which they always believed to lie in the foundations of life, that projects itself into the present in strange words and even stranger thoughts; such a future does not seem to them to be worth struggling for.

There is no fear more inhibiting than the fear of the future. Its effect on sensitive minds is profound. It pervades all the arts. It leads to a general disbelief in the efficacy of human intelligence, for if reason cannot offer a more pleasing prospect then it might be that reason itself is at fault.

This mood in its most extreme form found expression in fascism, which substituted a nostalgic irrationalism for the buoyant, robust and optimistic, bustling activity of the nineteenth and early twentieth centuries. The energy freed by the mechanical achievements of the Industrial Revolution was essentially outflowing. The surpluses of the advanced industrial nations invaded more and more areas of the world where economic and intellectual passivity had reigned for long centuries; and the spirit of the West responded to the challenge of the novel, the remote and the unknown.

Confidence in the ascendancy of human reason was confirmed by daily victories, especially in the physical sciences and the mechanical arts. It was not to be expected that the nature of the society that was being created should be a subject of contemplation, when all the time that society was pushing back its boundaries[24] and adding to its wealth. Contemplation and the introspective mood that is its congenial climate cannot be expected amidst the stridency and brashness of a revolution still obeying the thrust of its initial impulse.

Towards the end of the nineteenth century the trade unions of Britain began to gather new strength, and in the first decade of the twentieth century they burst into an angry roar of strikes and lockouts. The miners in particular gave the first few heaves of that prolonged protest which hastened the birth of the Labour Party and gave it many of its leaders.

In its attempt to harvest social discontents, the Liberal Party took the first few tentative steps towards the establishment of the social services, but these were too timid and hesitant to be really successful. The industrialists who were the chief backers of the Liberal Party were not prepared to allow any substantial part of their profits to be creamed off for welfare expenditure. It is the fashion of those who write history in the form of biographies to talk of the Liberal Party as having been destroyed by the personal ambitions of this or that leader, or as having been undermined by the intrigues of factions. These no doubt played their part. But by themselves they could never have led to the decline of the Liberal Party if history had still had an important role for it to play. The death of British Liberalism began when the Liberal administration of Mr Asquith came into collision with the dockers, the miners and the railwaymen. Subsequent quarrels among the Liberal leaders merely served to crack the outer shell. The kernel had begun to wither much earlier.

In these same years the rise of Germany and Japan as serious competitors for world markets that had long been dominated by Britain, began to cause a few anxious frowns and some foreboding. Self-questioning had begun. But it was a subordinate motif. It was not the prevailing mood.

In the main, Edwardian England displayed the buoyancy of social and intellectual self-confidence at its best. Its literature, its music, its general atmosphere, its lust for travel and exploration, were the final flowering of the process that started way back when the use of

steam power, coal and steel gave a powerful impetus to the accumulation of material wealth.

European society after the 1914–1918 war never recaptured that
mood. The awful slaughter of the war, and the epidemics that followed, produced a society that proved unequal to the problems
crowding in on it. The war had been in many respects a temporary
escape from economic problems that had now to be met in aggravated forms.[25]

The revolution in Russia posed questions for Europe that have
not yet been answered. The attack on China by Japan, and the prolonged civil war superimposed on external attack, posed not dis-
similar questions for all the nations entangled in the Orient. These
are being pressed with mounting urgency.

In Europe the past is dead. The future wears an ominous visage
for all who want to apply old remedies to new ailments. It was not
Socialism that killed the capitalist competitive societies of Europe.
They were killed by two world wars and by their failure to adapt
themselves to the economic conditions brought about by their own
agencies. At the moment they are floundering, unable to make up
their minds which way to choose. The assistance provided by the
United States does not enable them to recover. Rather it perpetuates
a spiritual languor. National mendicancy is no substitute for a
vigorous ambition.

In Great Britain the advent of a Labour government evoked hopes
that a solution might be found that was neither an attempt to resur-
rect what history had killed, nor yet a resort to political expedients
which had proved so grim in countries where more severe social
collisions had produced extreme reactions.

Democratic Socialism is not a middle way between capitalism and
Communism. If it were merely that, it would be doomed to failure
from the start. It cannot live by borrowed vitality. Its driving power
must derive from its own principles and the energy released by
them. It is based on the conviction that free men can use free
institutions to solve the social and economic problems of the day, if
they are given a chance to do so.

No Socialist would be so foolish as to underestimate the difficulties that beset him. If ever he were inclined to do so the post-war

period would have taught him differently. It was clear to the most ignorant that British industrial recovery after the war could be accomplished only by one of those supreme efforts which have more than once illumined our history. It was also clear to all but the shallow-minded, that this effort could be expected from the industrial masses only if the Government departed from the policies which had brought about British decline between the wars.

The country needed new men and new measures. It got both. The result was one of the most remarkable recoveries on record. Looking back over the period, it is now possible to see the chief reason for our success. It was self-confidence and the strength that comes from it. That self-confidence was founded in the belief that we knew what had to be done. The Labour majority in the House of Commons, after the General Election of 1945, had obtained from the country a clear mandate to carry out a number of measures which had been explained to the people in the election campaign and by intensive propaganda stretching over a number of decades. We were intellectually and spiritually armed for our task.

It is the practice of many publicists to sneer at the Labour Party for clinging to what are called 'doctrinaire' principles. You would imagine from the manner of these attacks that lack of principle is a suitable political equipment. No statesman can stand the strain of modern political life without the inner serenity that comes from fidelity to a number of guiding convictions. Without their steadying influence he is blown about by every passing breeze. Nor is cleverness and political agility a substitute for them. It has always been for me a painful spectacle when some Labour spokesman tries to justify a piece of Socialist legislation on exclusively 'practical' grounds. There are at least two considerations to be kept in mind when making policy: its applicability to the immediate situation certainly, but also its faithfulness to the general body of principles which make up your philosophy. Without the latter, politics is merely a job like any other.

Nor is it possible to steer a steady course unless you have a clear vision of the destination you are making for. There are always influences at work trying to blur issues and sap your faith. The

Labour movement does not live in a vacuum. The defeatism that accompanies the decline of the old social order seeps in from every direction. There are too many Conservatives who have not the courage to apply their Conservative principles, and too many Socialists afraid of their Socialism. A nation too long suspended between alternative courses of action is in a sorry plight. It is even worse when we can discern little difference between the parties seeking our suffrage. We are not there yet, but there is a danger that we shall get there if recent tendencies are not corrected.

Then there is the disposition to smooth away the edges of policy in the hope of making it more attractive to doubtful supporters. It is better to risk a clear and definite rejection than to win uneasy followers by dexterous ambiguities.

Whenever the Labour Party has made a mistake, it has not been in consequence of pursuing its principles too roughly or too far, but by making too many concessions to conventional opinion. An illustration of this is to be found in the nationalized industries. We allowed ourselves to be frightened away from the clear application of our policy by the clamour of the Press about the dangers of putting civil servants in charge of great industries. We entrusted these industries to boards, leaving only a power of general direction to the Ministers. The argument went that no Minister could possibly be responsible for all the details of administration, and that if he tried to do so the result would be delay in reaching decisions and endless red tape. One of the causes of this reasoning is the folklore that has grown up around private enterprise. The assumption is that the modern business man manages all the details of his business, large or small, and that the thrust of his inspired personality is felt from the boardroom to the office boy. The fact is, of course, that there is at least as much danger of a rigid bureaucracy in private as in public administration. Remote control is the consequence of bigness, not of the nature of the ownership.

The principles of good administration are the same in all forms of organization. If that were not so it would be impossible to justify the appointment of the same men as directors of so many and widely differing concerns. They cannot possibly be familiar with the technical details. What they do know, or at least they should know, are the administrative mechanisms by means of which the businesses are kept efficient and authority delegated to where it belongs.

There is no fundamental difference between the National Health Service and the railways in terms of administration. There are more than three hundred thousand health workers for whom the Minister of Health is responsible to Parliament. When the Health Service was formed, and it was known that I intended to be answerable directly to the House of Commons, I was warned that I would be overwhelmed by questions ranging from purely personal inquiries to wide issues of policy. The fears proved in practice to be without justification. The right to question the Minister of Health is an invaluable instrument for keeping the Health Service vigorous and up to date. Most Members of Parliament soon learned to distinguish between trivial and really important questions.

The trouble with the boards of the nationalized industries is that they are a constitutional outrage. It is not proper that a Member of Parliament should be expected to defer to a non-elected person. The Minister, by divesting himself of parliamentary responsibility, disfranchises the House of Commons; and that means he disfranchises the electorate as well.

Part of the case for public ownership is public accountability. This can be effectively provided only if the Minister concerned can be questioned in the House. The present state of affairs reduces the Minister to the status of either a messenger or an apologist for the boards. This was a mistake for which I must accept my share of responsibility.

But the boards of our nationalized industries, in their present form, are a new and potentially dangerous problem, both constitutionally and socially. We have still to ensure that they are taking us towards Democratic Socialism, not towards the managerial society.

There is a disposition in some quarters to believe that the latter is the next stage in social evolution. That would be to surrender to the worst feature of the Great Society – its impersonal character. Over and over again I have laid stress on the need to make the citizen the master of his social environment. No real progress is made if the new order leaves him the passive creature of a class of supposed supermen, even though these present themselves in the guise of public servants.

In my short experience as Minister of Labour I was made aware of this lamentable tendency. The statutory immunity of the boards of nationalized industries from direct parliamentary control feeds this psychology. This makes it all the more necessary that the statutes should be revised.

The conversion of an industry to public ownership is only the first step towards Socialism. It is an all-important step, for without it the conditions of further progress are not established. One important consequence is a shift of power that resolves the conflict between public and private claims. The danger of the state machine being manipulated by private vested interests is thus reduced. An additional result, and one of the greatest importance, is that the nationalized industry is available as a direct instrument of economic planning. It is no longer necessary to rely on a complicated system of financial inducements as, for instance, in dealing with backward textile firms: these had to be bribed to put in modern machinery, and even so the bribes were only partially successful. Contrast this with the development plans of the National Coal Board[26] and of the British Electricity Authority, and with the development of the gas grid. There are other important benefits accruing to the community from enlarging public ownership, but these fall in their proper place in a later chapter.

The advance from state ownership to full Socialism is in direct proportion to the extent the workers in the nationalized sector are made aware of a changed relationship between themselves and the management. The persistence of a sense of dualism in a publicly owned industry is evidence of an immature industrial democracy. It means that emotionally the 'management' is still associated with the conception of alien ownership, and the 'workers' are still 'hands'.

Until we make the cross-over to a spirit of co-operation, the latent energies of democratic participation cannot be fully released; nor shall we witness that spiritual homogeneity that comes when the workman is united once more with the tools of his craft, a unity that was ruptured by the rise of economic classes. The individual citizen

the butcher's boy (left white coat)

the young miners' leader

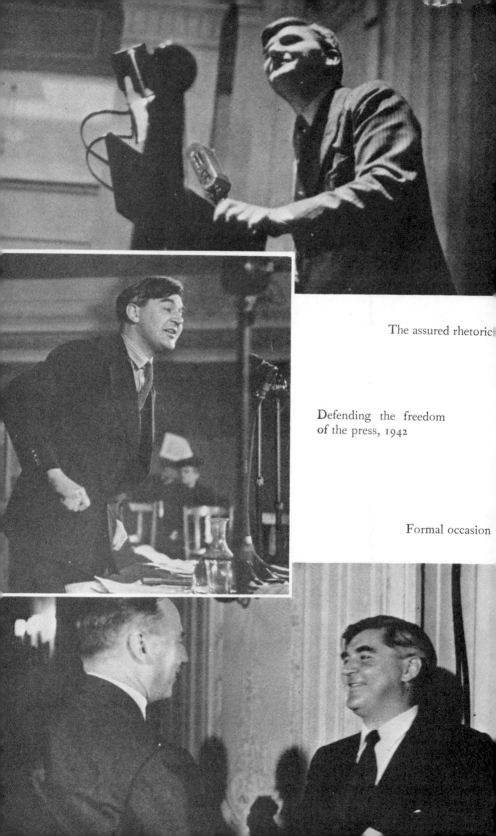

The assured rhetoric

Defending the freedom of the press, 1942

Formal occasion

Minister of Health

Minister
of Labour

Off duty

At the Branch Meeting

Talking:

Labour Party Conference, 1955

Listening:

A press conference

With Nenni and Mendés-France,
as seen by Cartier-Bresson

An essay in restraint; addressing the Trafalgar Square rally at the Suez crisis, 1956

Opening a health exhibition, 1956

Entertaining Continental socialists

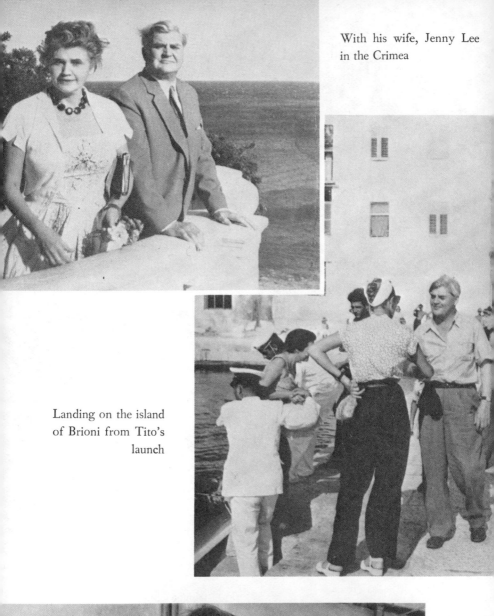

With his wife, Jenny Lee in the Crimea

Landing on the island of Brioni from Tito's launch

Sailing in Adriatic i holiday m 1952

will still feel that society is on top of him until he is enfranchised in the workshop as well as at the ballot box.

Indeed, vital though it is, ballot-box democracy at municipal and national elections is limited and only partially satisfactory, because it is occasional and remote instead of continuous and intimate.

It will take time to break down the antagonisms between worker and management – time, patience and infinite ingenuity. The psychology of belligerency is the legacy of old struggles and fears. Which is the more productive? The discipline of fear or the sustained energy of confidence? Conservative thinking relies mainly on the fear of dismissal as the most effective form of discipline in the workshop. But fear is inhibiting and wasteful, not releasing and fertile. In so far as fear of punishment is an effective discipline, it is appropriate only to primitive mass gang operations under the vigilant, ever-watchful eye of the foreman. It is less and less effective as mental co-operation becomes as important as simple physical effort.

Nor is the situation rendered so different when the worker is attached to the conveyor belt and other forms of repetitive industry. This induces only a dull resentment and a torpid attitude in the worker unless some way is found to give him a wider place in policy and management than is afforded by making him a mere automatic appendage to a machine.

The more the division of labour makes the worker a cog in the machine the more essential it is to refresh his mind and spirit by the utmost discussion and consultation in policy and administration. Where this has been tried with a real will to make it work, executive action has not been impaired. On the contrary, the worker goes more than half-way to carry out decisions that are the clear result of carefully explained plans. The very necessity for allotting to the individual worker a small part in the productive process, requires that he sees its overall relationship to the general scheme.:

Many, though not all, managements in the nationalized industries, approached their task with a heightened fear that the workers would prove even less amenable to necessary disciplines now that they were working in their own industries. This led them to emphasize that nothing had really changed. By this attitude they robbed themselves

E

at the outset of the opportunity to engage the interest and affections of the workers. It was stupid and unimaginative. It follows, of course, from having to continue to engage executives who were in many cases hostile to the change that had been brought about.

The methods of promotion in the publicly owned industries will have to be carefully scrutinized or we shall find the defects of some of the existing managers reproduced in their appointees. A new class of manager must be trained and he must be taught that we are not building a new species of pyramid. The crack of the overseer's whip, however disguised in its modern form, is not how Socialists see the future of industrial relations. We have not come thus far merely in order to slip into a new kind of industrial helotry.

Each freedom is made safe only by adding another to it. Democracy is protected by extending its boundaries. The emergence of modern industry, with its danger of depersonalization of the worker, challenges the vitality of democratic principles. In the societies of the West, industrial democracy is the counterpart of political freedom. Liberty and responsibility march together. They must be joined together in the workshop as in the legislative assembly. Only when this is accomplished shall we have the foundations of a buoyant and stable civilization.

NOTE 24

Between 1876 and 1900, Britain added 576,334 square miles to her colonial possessions in Asia and 3,279,934 square miles to those she already held in Africa. In these two continents there were approximately 110 million more people under British colonial rule in 1900 than in 1876. Though being rapidly overtaken by the United States and Germany, with whom she found it increasingly difficult to compete, Britain almost doubled her exports during this period.

NOTE 25

The figures for industrial production quoted in Note 17, Chapter Four, make this abundantly clear to all save those in whom political prejudice has produced a complete insensitivity to fact. The further fact that by

1926, eight years after World War I, British manufacturing industry under
'free enterprise' was still producing 21.2 per cent *less* than in 1913 (see
A Survey of the Economic Situation and Prospects of Europe. New York:
United Nations, 1948), is therefore added for chastening effect.

There are some British citizens who seek, however, to decry their own
country's efforts under a Labour government by adverse comparisons
with the achievements of the United States. The following figures, taken
from *Facts About the British Economy* (E.C.A. Mission to the United
Kingdom, February 1950), put this matter into better perspective:

	Industrial Production	
	United States	United Kingdom
Year	*(1934–9 = 100)*	*(1934–8 = 100)*
1943	239	126
1946	170	104
1947	187	112
1948	192	125
1949	180	133

The colossal increase in the United States of 129 per cent in 1943 above
pre-war levels, as compared with the more modest increase of 26 per cent
in Britain, is clearly a reflection of the stimulus given to American
industry by a division of the war effort which gave the United States the
overwhelming preponderance of the war-production task. With the
advent of peace her industrial production index dropped by 69 points
against Britain's 22 point decline. But from 1946–9 the improvement was
10 points in the case of the United States and 29 points in the United
Kingdom.

While these figures, taken from different year bases, must be taken with
appropriate caution, it is plain that Britain, who had been denied the
wartime stimulus to her industries and whose peacetime industrial
equipment had been allowed to become obsolete and worn out, has made
a remarkable recovery effort – even in comparison with America. The
E.C.A. Mission to Britain evidently thought so, for it reported as follows:

'The rate of British improvement in industrial output in the post-
war years compares favourably with that of the United States, even
between 1946 and 1948. Moreover, the recession which lowered United

States industrial output in 1949 did not affect the rising trend of British production.'

On Britain's agricultural industry's achievements the E.C.A. reported as follows:

'In the United States, agricultural production has risen since 1947 by 6 per cent, while the most comparable United Kingdom index, net output, shows and increase of nearly 9 per cent (net output reflects the increased production out of Britain's own resources, and economies made in the use of imported foods, etc.). In both the United States and the United Kingdom, 1949 production is not only well above pre-war, but, quite significantly, has remained at around the high war-time levels.'

Most people, apart from the more raucous sections of the British Conservative Party, now take some pride in Britain's post-war production efforts.

NOTE 26
Plan for Coal (published by the National Coal Board in October 1950, and obtainable through British Information Services in the United States), is a remarkable document which will repay careful study. If the pre-war British coal industry had tackled its problems with half the thoroughness displayed by the National Coal Board since nationalization, our whole national economy would have been in a much stronger and more independent position than it is today.

7

Social Tensions

THE safety of free political institutions depends upon resolving social tensions before these become intolerable. In a society where the bulk of property is privately owned, public spending is always an invasion of private rights. The product of industry is distributed in the form of money incomes: as interest, profits, rents, wages and salaries. The proportion of the product retained by industrial corporations and private concerns, apart from what is needed for replacement of wasted assets, is merely postponed dividends.

At this stage there is no money in the possession of public authorities, national and municipal. Private enterprise first puts the national income in private pockets: then public spending becomes possible only by taking back some portion of the private income by means of rates and taxes. There is, therefore, an obvious conflict between what is needed for public purposes, and the inclination of the individual to keep as much as possible for himself. This statement can be qualified, refined and varied in many ways, but in the main it is a true description of what takes place.

Many of the political tensions in individualist society come from this source. Where the requirements of public spending are modest, the conflict produces little political strain. But it is otherwise when the demands of public expenditure result in clawing back a significant proportion of private income.[27] At this stage tax resistance shows itself and the temperature of political controversy is heightened.

The strains so created are all the more intense because the objects of public spending commend themselves to the conscience of the majority of the nation. These include national defence as well as the various social services that enlightened opinion has caused the nation to adopt. The individual who is called on to alienate a painful part of his private income to the tax collector is not made any the more willing because it is going to finance purposes it is not easy for him to condemn. In public he is often ready enough to applaud the objects for which his money is required. He becomes a sort of Jekyll and Hyde. As Jekyll, the good citizen, he is pleased that his country should provide education, old age pensions, service pensions, widows' pensions, health services, an effective defence force and so on. But as Hyde, the individual taxpayer, he resents paying the bill.

The political consequences of this situation vary from nation to nation. In some continental countries it is notoriously difficult to collect taxes justly. Certain political parties find it impossible to face the results of insisting on effective collection of taxes. In France, in Italy, and now in the United States of America, wholesale evasion of taxes has become a problem for the governments concerned. As modern industry produces new and attractive forms of private consumption, the individual citizen is made all the more reluctant to see his income taken away from him for remote purposes. It is here that an elementary selection of priorities is seen to be at variance with the values of an acquisitive society. Great Britain has long enjoyed the reputation of a nation where people pay their taxes, if not enthusiastically, at least honestly. Yet even here the tensions created by the high incidence of taxation caused the Labour Party to acquiesce in a charge on the Health Service rather than an increase in taxes. In France and Italy not even the imperious needs of national defence have sufficed to discipline the property-owning classes into accepting a significant reduction of their private expenditure.

The conflict between the demands of public spending and the general class of taxpayer is further aggravated by the knowledge that many are able to escape their just share of taxes. The income of wage and salary earners and of most of the professional classes is known, and the revenue office takes the full amount the law demands. But many members of the trading and business community escape proper payment by concealing their real earnings. Prospective employees in the administrative departments of businesses quite commonly ask that part of their remuneration be paid as an expense allowance, and this is not unusually granted. Many in command of businesses are adept at the art of charging their businesses with their private living expenses.

It is in the realm of cash trading, however, that the greatest evasion of taxation occurs. It is well nigh impossible for the revenue officer to assess the amount of cash transactions that occur between individuals. Payment by cheque is almost an affront in certain lines of business. The spiv (petty black-market operator) has entered into modern literature not only as a by-product of a rationing system. He is the modern equivalent of the smuggler. He is the prototype of the evader of taxes. All this occasions the bitterest resentment among those citizens whose social situation forces them to pay in full.

The consequences from a Socialist point of view of what really amounts to a penalization of the honest and of those whose job does not permit evasion is exceedingly serious. The power and prosperity of tax evaders thwarts one of the main aims of Socialism: the establishment of just, social relationships.

It is not my intention to write a treatise on tax evasion. I mention it at such length because it underlines a significant shift of values in modern society. Orthodox Socialism believed in direct taxation. I listened to Lord Snowden on many occasions explaining its virtues. It never seemed to occur to him that there was a definite limit to taxation as a means of redistributing wealth; and as a device for financing expanding social services. I must not be thought to hold the view that additional taxes are not possible among certain classes. Of course they are; but they will not serve to resolve the deep antagonism between public and private spending that now holds the centre of the political stage.

Unless a radical solution is found, the political parties will tend to revolve around the ridiculous issue of sixpence on or off the income tax. This is purely Liberal polemics. In these circumstances the social services become a political football, kicked about from one election to another. The individual finds his most selfish instincts mobilized against any reasonable order of social priorities, and politics degenerate into a squalid round of catchpenny propaganda.

No student of politics would deny that this is a real dilemma; and it is always implicit in *laissez-faire* society. As I have already said, where the property-owning classes believe that the function of disposing of the economic surplus should lie with them, there is bound to be resentment when the state steps in and takes some of the surplus for its own purposes. This is the conflict in society as a whole. It is a national facet of the hundred and one conflicts between wages and profits. The struggle is for the economic surplus, and not only for a share of the increased wealth which follows from greater productivity. It is a demand for more equality in the distribution of existing wealth, and for a say in what is to happen to the increment.

When state activity expands as at present, as a consequence of rearmament and of the extension of the social services, the share of the national income taken by the state makes a harsh impact on individual plans and ambitions.

The perils of inflation,[28] ever threatening in conditions of full employment where most of the economy is privately owned, add further inflammable material to the political scene. Those whose property appreciates in value and who are able to dispose of some of it, or borrow on it, do so, and thus maintain their personal expenditure. This gives an additional impulse to rising prices. The wage and salary earners try to recoup themselves by a revision of their contracts with their employers, and so high prices are pushed higher.

In the meantime, those with fixed incomes are left behind in the race. Where these are recipients of state pensions, old age pensioners, ex-servicemen, widows, and the like, they naturally bring pressure to bear on their political representatives, and a tense political situation is made tenser.

The behaviour of the political parties in these circumstances corresponds to the character of the people from whom they get most support. It is this behaviour which indicates the nature of the class alignment in society. In times of crisis the Conservative Party invariably attacks state expenditure on the social services so as to relieve the burden on property. The Socialist Party, on the other hand, rushes to the defence of state spending: their supporters are the poor and the defenceless who most need it. The resulting legislation obeys these pressures, modified only by fear of what may happen when next the parties face the electorate.

It is manifestly unfair that those whom the community selected
for special help and protection should suffer because of rising prices.
It is not that the nation as a whole is poorer. Even if it were, the
weakest should not bear the brunt. If real property can avail itself of
ways of cancelling the effect of rising prices, why should not those
who have to seek the help of the social services be able to obtain
redress, without having to resort to political pressures that must at
best succeed only after delayed action?

There seems no reason why the cost-of-living index, when
brought up to date, should not be used for the purpose of readjust-
ing the scales of benefits, say at six-month intervals. I am not here
discussing improvements in their standards. What is first required
is that the existing standards be defended and this by a method which
would work automatically without necessitating a series of parliamentary crises. At one stroke, one cause of political tension would
be removed.

If the reply is made that the principle should work both ways,
and that the scale of benefits should be adjusted downwards with a
fall in prices, there are two answers. There is little or no prospect of
a general fall in the prices of the goods that go to the making of the
cost-of-living index. As far as we can see we are in for a steady
upward trend in prices. We shall be lucky if it is steady. If, however,
a fall does take place, the increased purchasing power resulting to
the beneficiaries of the social services would be a useful means of
defence against deflation and consequent unemployment.

The same principle should apply to national savings certificates.[29]
The present practice is not fair: and it is unfair at the expense of
some of the most deserving. The vast majority of those who buy
these certificates, do so partly as an insurance against a family
financial emergency, or in order to provide little graces and urbani-
ties to their lives when they retire.

For the most part they are not familiar with the complexities of
the stock exchange and the money market. They are little people,
artists, scientists, professional and other workers, too pre-occupied
with their work to give time and attention to the world of the
money changers, or disinclined to do so. They do not look on their
savings as an investment. but as a cushion. It is unjust that they lend

*E

to the state the savings that represent so much sacrifice, and get back a sum which in real purchasing power is substantially less than they lent. If the value of their savings could be protected, they would probably be prepared to accept a lower rate of interest: for, I repeat, it is not the income from the savings that plays the greater part in their minds, but the savings themselves.

The application of this principle would have the effect of easing the inflationary pressure, for people are more inclined to buy goods than to tie up their money in paper claims that have a declining value.

The reader will note that I have been arguing for the introduction of the principle of automatism in certain branches of our social and political life. It is part of my general contention that it should not be necessary for individuals to make so many convulsive efforts in order to keep abreast of a changing social environment. These make our lives too unpredictable and tumultuous, and exclude the hope of more serenity in man's relations with society.

I believe it is now necessary to apply the same principle to a wider and even more controversial field. The workers' attitude to the national income as expressed through their trade unions falls roughly under two heads: first, a demand for a more just apportionment of the total social product; and second, a fair share of the result of increased productivity. The struggle to attain both of these is obscured by a third element: the effort to defend their standard of living in a time of rising prices.

If we could once secure that real wages are not eaten into by rises in the cost of living, the way would be clearer to a national wages policy. Most people who have given their minds to the problem are now convinced that a national wages policy is an inevitable corollary of full employment, if we are not to be engulfed by inflation. A lot of hard thinking and perhaps harder talking will be required before we win through to something of a permanently satisfactory nature.

The first essential is to stop the ground from slipping under our feet. It should not be beyond our collective good sense to apply the reformed cost of living index to the whole field of wages and salaries. The question, as I know full well, is at what point to set the date line. The trade union world is involved in a continuous succession of wage negotiations. Each union is naturally disinclined to adopt any general principle until its own particular negotiations have been completed. Before that point is reached, other unions have put in fresh wage claims, so at no stage can it be said that a holding-line has been arrived at.

It is no use railing at the union leaders, for their difficulties are real and perplexing. Nevertheless, a new departure will have to be made if the British economy is not to plunge from a condition of unbalance into a fatal tail spin.

Once we can reach universal acceptance of a cost-of-living index, the principle of automatism will help tranquillize the whole of industry, and the way will be clear to tackle the next part of the problem, which is the extent of the economic increment, if any, and how to distribute it over the whole system in the form of improved standards.

No one can pretend that the labour force of Britain is at present distributed in a fashion that takes account of urgent national priorities; and the impact of rearmament will worsen the position beyond the imaginings of many whose complacency thrives on an unawareness of the facts. The continued failure of the coal mines to attract a sufficient labour force is* conclusive evidence of the counter-attraction of other and much less urgent occupations.

The introduction of Italian labour into the mines is not a solution. It is merely an escape from present headaches and a precursor of worse ones to come. In our crowded island no one should pretend that a shortage of labour in a particular industry is solved by bringing workers in from abroad. The problem is one of maldistribution of our labour force, and this, in its turn, is the consequence of a capital and wages policy that obeys no long-term purposive intention.

In the absence of a policy which strictly relates current adjustments of personal incomes to any surplus which may be available for distribution, mounting paper claims will continue to produce a series of crises both in industry and in politics until bewilderment generates despair, and despair in its turn sinks into apathy.

*In 1938 the total number of wage earners on colliery books was 782,000. In July 1951 the figure was 701,000.

These suggestions in no way solve the problem posed at the beginning of this chapter. On the contrary, they serve to intensify it. If the real value of public spending is preserved by automatic adjustments following movements in the cost-of-living index, the burden of taxation is the same. The money figure will be higher, but the effect in goods and services will be the same. My purpose is to secure that earned income along with the social services and small savings shall not be mulcted, thus shifting the burden from unearned income and real property. There is a real dilemma in that the more you protect some people from inflation, the greater the sacrifice from those who are unprotected and the faster the rise in prices. We need in fact safety valves built into the economy, and if one of them is removed (for instance, the present vulnerability of the small rentier and pensioner), then others, for example a cost-of-living index that underweighs luxuries, must be provided. The value of this approach is that it would minimize the political strain that follows from one class after another attempting to catch up with the fall in the purchasing power of money.

I am not here dealing with the problems arising from trading relations between Britain and the rest of the world. One of the results of world inflation has been to reduce imports by making it harder for people to buy at the higher prices. This is the automatism of the price system. If men and women were themselves automatons it might still work. But they are not. Long before the price mechanism is able to effect the results expected of it, political pressures and industrial action get to work. This has long been recognized. The method now resorted to is direct intervention by the state to prevent the import of less wanted goods. This is one more example of the incompatibility of political democracy and the price mechanism of the competitive system. If people were not free to compel the recovery of their real incomes, the price mechanism would bring about equilibrium after considerable suffering by the poor. The price mechanism requires the abolition of democratic institutions for its smooth operation.

The question I am now considering is the political one which emerges when a high rate of public spending begins to produce tax resistance and evasion on a wide and socially damaging scale.

No solution would be satisfactory to a Socialist which merely produced a lower rate of taxation, for this would be at the expense of the poorer members of the community. A fiscal solution is therefore impossible. We must search in other directions.

The chief cause of our difficulty lies in the fact that the whole national product is distributed in the form of money incomes of various kinds and then the state has to get some of it back. This is not merely because industry is in the main in private hands, but because private property is exceedingly badly distributed. Once a larger proportion of industry is publicly owned, a larger part of public spending could be financed out of the surplus which now accrues to private owners. While it would be unfair to tax the consumers of nationalized industries or services specially hard by increasing the price of nationalized goods and services for this purpose, it is equally wrong to stimulate the consumption, sometimes the wasteful consumption, of these goods by fixing their price below the true cost of production. For example, the less favoured colliery areas work at a loss at a time when every piece of coal is precious.

If there are special reasons for providing goods or services, whether nationalized or otherwise, below the cost of production, that should be decided upon on special grounds.

In general, the fact that an industry is nationalized should provide additional income to the state, for, among other reasons, compensation is paid at a low rate of interest on gilt-edged securities while the profit rate extracted in private concerns is usually much higher. As we move away from the period when compensation is first paid, the financial advantages increase. The surpluses from these communally owned industries would accrue to the national exchequer and taxation could be correspondingly reduced. This would not mean that taxpayers would have more money to spend. As we have seen, this could only be done by hurting the recipients of public benefits. But it would mean that more of what was distributed in the form of private income could in the main be privately spent, and the individual would be spared the pain of seeing so much taken from him that he thought was his to spend.[30]

I am not suggesting the abolition of income tax. That would only be possible if all industries belonged to the community, for then taxation would take the form of the state share of the industrial product. But in order to be able to reduce inequalities in income we should institute a far-reaching capital levy. Until recently, death duties were supposed to bring this about and to do so with less administrative difficulty. But inequality in the distribution of wealth has hardly decreased: death duties can be evaded through trusts and gifts. The appreciation of capital assets, and of the value of shares through the ploughing back of profits (which also enables the evasion of surtax) must also be taken into account.

We have, therefore, still to devise a system that works with maximum fairness and the least political tension. This can only be done if the individual is not made the enemy of all decent social activities every time the tax collector calls.

A number of invaluable social consequences would immediately flow from the situation thus created. There would be less cheating of the revenue officer, for the incomes of workers in nationalized industries are known. Cash transactions would be confined to the smaller private sector of industry. The possibilities of tax evasion would be reduced in this sector, for part of the cost of maintaining public expenditure would have been transferred to the price of the products of the nationalized industries; and, of course, the cost-of-living index would not apply to the rate of profit.

A further consequence would be a lessening of the inflationary pressure. The property of the socialized industries could not be sold privately or borrowed on for private spending. We all know that much of the private spending that now occurs comes from continuous capital appreciation, and from capital gains. Such private capital as the nationalized industries required would be in the form of fixed interest-bearing stock. Whether some protection would be required for it is a matter for consideration.

Then again, additional wealth created by the expansion of the nationalized industries, could not be creamed off from time to time as is the case in private industry when speculators take their capital gains.

The inflationary pressure in Britain would be much more than it is today were it not for the transfer to public ownership of coal, gas, steel, electricity, cables and wireless. This is probably one of the chief reasons why Britain, though hard pressed, has not suffered the same inflation as other countries where the whole of industry is open to the gambler, the money-lender and the taker of quick gains.

The facilities given to national planning when industries are publicly owned are obvious. Control and direction of investment is easier, and a more secure market is provided for the private industries. These are the main consumers of the products of the nationalized industries. Each time an attempt has to be made to mobilize the resources of the nation for some central purpose, whether it be an export drive in particular markets or a spurt in arming, the same planning difficulties are experienced; private business offers up resistance at a thousand and one points. Controls of various kinds have to be resorted to; pivotal raw materials carefully canalized to where they are most required; licences given or withheld; all requiring the employment of tens of thousands of men and women not only to administer them but also to see that private business does not cheat or corrupt the state officials. The work of this army of officials is not directly productive. It is the price we have to pay for competitive individualism whenever we try to force it to serve some other purpose than its own view of its interest.

If the public domain of industry were large enough to influence the conduct of the rest, most of these direct and indirect controls and regulations would not be needed, and the men and women running them could be released for productive work.

If I am told that these controls over private enterprise were only temporary, I answer that as far as Britain in concerned, state direction of our economy in one form or another has come to stay, and it might as well stay in a respectable fashion by a radical extension of public ownership. The Conservative government elected in Britain in the autumn of 1951, found itself faced with the necessity of imposing even more controls over industry than it had inherited from its Labour predecessors.

I doubt whether even the United States will ever be able completely to dismantle the system of state regulations she has been forced to adopt for the arms programme. If she is ever tempted to do

so, she had better take a careful look round the raw material situation[31] before giving full steam ahead to any kind of production
American business might find temporarily attractive. The world
might not be able to afford another spate of thoughtless and wasteful
production similar to that which we have experienced during the
last fifty years. If the American economy cannot control itself, parts
of the rest of the world might have to protect its own raw material
resources from early exhaustion.

To steer a wholly private enterprise economy in a given direction
for any considerable length of time is practically impossible. It is
alien to the laws of its being. It engenders not only the tensions I
have been describing but also a universal furtiveness as individuals
seek to pursue their own personal adventures in business and
finance. A British Minister of the Crown, when asked how people
were to get steel, replied, 'Scrounge for it.' That mood may be tolerable for a short time. As a permanent economic climate it is
unendurable.

Thus, judged from any angle, the relations between public and
private enterprise have not yet reached a condition where they can
be stabilized. That is why it is so foolish for certain Labour men to
preach 'consolidation' at this stage. Before we can dream of consolidation, the power relations of public and private property must
be drastically altered. The solution of the problems I have been
discussing cannot be approached until it becomes possible to create
a purposive and intelligible design for society. That cannot be done
until effective social and economic power passes from one order of
society to another.

At the moment we are between two worlds. We have lost the
propulsions of one and we have not yet gained the forward thrust
of the other. This is no place in which to halt.

That is not to say a halting place cannot be reached. I think it can.
It is clear to the serious student of modern politics that a mixed
economy is what most people of the West would prefer. The victory
of Socialism need not be universal to be decisive. I have no patience
with those Socialists, so-called, who in practice would socialize
nothing, while in theory they threaten the whole of private property.
They are purists and therefore barren. It is neither prudent, nor does

it accord with our conception of the future, that all forms of private property should live under perpetual threat. In almost all types of human society different forms of property have lived side by side without fatal consequences either for society or for one of them. But it is a requisite of social stability that one type of property ownership should dominate. In the society of the future it should be public property. Private property should yield to the point where social purposes and a decent order of priorities form an easily discernible pattern of life. Only when this is accomplished will a tranquil and serene attitude take the place of the all-pervading restlessness that is the normal climate of competitive society.

Where the frontier between the public and private sector should be fixed is a question that will be answered differently in different nations, according to their traditions and stage of historical development. In countries with a primitive economic development where revolutions have occurred, it is natural that industries will tend to grow up in the public domain. This was the case in Russia, and it will almost certainly be so in the new China. Progress is not a spiral. It is rather a kind of zigzag movement as nations are influenced in their formative period by the ideas and institutions of other nations impinging upon them. It is natural that the Orient should be influenced by the collectivist ideas of Soviet Russia rather than by Western conceptions of progress; though it is to be hoped that the results in the U.S.S.R. of a monolithic and centralized collectivism will induce modifications and variations of the collectivist philosophy, as is now the case in Yugoslavia.

In the Western world the extension of the principles of public ownership will be influenced by the extent to which large aggregations of private capital have coagulated into monopolies and semi-monopolies in which profit is a clear tax on the community and no longer a reward for risk.

So, also, the existence of producer and consumer co-operatives may be expected to exert their influence on the character and direction of the public domain.

NOTE 27

As for example in Britain since the end of World War II. See the figures reproduced below from Table 13 of *National Income and Expenditure of the United Kingdom, 1946–50* (Cmd. 8203. H.M.S.O., 1951):

Proportion of Personal Income Required to Meet Taxation
£ million

	1938	1948	1949	1950
Personal Income	4,952	9,999	10,507	11,042
Provision for taxes on income and national insurance contributions	415	1,413	1,559	1,589
Indirect taxes on consumption	578	1,919	1,852	1,904
Less subsidies to consumption	–35	–553	–506	–468
Total tax liabilities in respect of personal income	958	2,779	2,905	3,025
Tax liabilities as a percentage of personal income	19	28	28	27

From the above table it is possible to calculate the percentage taken from personal incomes by way of direct taxes (i.e. income tax and surtax): in 1938, 9 per cent; in 1948, 14 per cent; in 1949, 15 per cent; in 1950, 15 per cent.

The above figures relate, however, to the nation as a whole. The amounts deducted from personal incomes by way of direct taxes on income are therefore shown below classified according to various income groupings – for 1938 and 1949 respectively.

Ranges of income before tax.	1938 Proportion of Income deducted with Taxes at 1938–9 rates	1949 Proportion of Income deducted with Taxes at 1949–50 rates
Under £250 per annum	0.2%	1.1%
£250–£499	3.2%	5.3%
£500–£999	10.8%	14.8%
£1,000–£1,999	18.2%	26.0%
£2,000–£9,999	29.1%	42.6%
£10,000 and over	57.7%	76.8%

Among the lower income groups the changes since 1938 have not been of undue significance. In any event these are the principal beneficiaries of the food subsidies. But the increases of direct taxation are of much more importance in the case of the middle income groups and effect, in particular, the professional classes, salaried executives and the like.

NOTE 28

The internal purchasing power of the pound sterling was 14s 3d in October 1951, as compared with the average of 20s in 1945. (The Chancellor of the Exchequer in answer to a Parliamentary question on 4 December, 1951. *Parliamentary Debates* [Hansard], House of Commons, Vol. 494, col. 209.)

NOTE 29

The capital and interest of a national savings certificate purchased in July 1945 for 15s, after making allowance for the fall in the internal purchasing power of the pound, was worth about 13s in October 1951. (The Chancellor of the Exchequer, in an answer to a Parliamentary question on 4 December, 1951. *Parliamentary Debates* [Hansard], House of Commons, Vol. 494, Col. 209.)

NOTE 30

I prefer an element of taxation in the prices paid for the goods and services provided by an extended range of nationalized industries to the currently imposed Purchase Taxes. These serve their purpose in that they give the individual an apparent freedom to spend his income (after deduction of direct taxes) as he wishes. But they involve an army of officials, and their computation and collection is a cause of much clerical and non-productive labour which could be used to better effect.

NOTE 31

The approaching exhaustion of the known supplies of many vital raw materials was discussed at the United Nations Scientific Conference on the Conservation and Utilization of Resources held from 17 August to 6 September, 1949, at Lake Success, New York. Critical mineral shortages were disclosed, for example, by Mr H. L. Keenleyside, Deputy

Minister, Department of Mines and Resources, Canada, in a speech
delivered on 18 August, 1949, from which the following extract is taken:

'Scientists and industrialists agree on the necessity of maintaining an
ample supply of minerals and metals if contemporary forms of civilization are to be maintained, or if further progress is to be achieved along
lines aready defined. Iron, copper, lead, zinc, nickel, aluminium,
magnesium and other base metals are by definition fundamental to our
way of life. Almost equally important are such alloying metals as
manganese, chromium, molybdenum and tungsten, which are essential
to the steel industry. The industrial minerals – limestone, sulphur, salt
and fluorspar – supply the raw materials for much of the world's
chemical industry, while the mineral fertilizers, phosphate rock and
potash, are of growing importance in agriculture. Without these, or of
effective substitutes, large segments of the prospective population on
the earth will be condemned to misery and degradation.

'Since the beginning of this century the depletion of our mineral
resources has been proceeding at an unexampled rate. Indeed the
quantity of mineral products consumed between 1900 and 1949 far
exceeds that of the whole preceding period of man's existence on earth.
It is a grim commentary on human intelligence that a great proportion
of the minerals used during the last five decades has been criminally
wasted in the waging of the most destructive wars in history.

'It is quite clear that the combination of an increasing population and
rising standards of living will place a strain on our metal reserves which
will almost certainly in the end prove beyond the capacity of man and
nature to supply.'

8

World Leadership

ONE of the difficulties of international intercourse is that it is almost impossible to express critical views about the policy of a nation to which you do not belong, without exposing yourself to the charge of being 'anti' that nation. This reaction is fed by a wide assortment of newspaper editorial writers and columnists, and, of course, by the statesmen whose politics are criticized. Now if there is one thing I find objectionable it is generalizing about whole peoples. There are no doubt 'noble' or 'ignoble', 'servile' or 'courageous' individuals, but when we apply such adjectives to nations, and groups within nations, what we are in fact doing is describing our own emotional reactions to conduct which meets with our approval or disapproval.

The danger of such language is its very effectiveness. It transfers to the nation concerned emotional connotations that belong to the world of personal relations. From that point on, rational and objective discussion about national policies is conducted in an atmosphere charged with prejudice.

I write this with no real belief that it will exempt me from misrepresentation by those whose job it is to misrepresent. All I seek to do is to put the unbiased reader on his guard. The intrinsic difficulties of the issues set out in this chapter are sufficiently serious without the added encumbrance of confusing personal and national reactions.

When the Second World War ended there was great anxiety in Europe lest the U.S.A. should once more retire into isolationism. I did not share this fear, for it did not seem to me to accord either with the facts of her economic relations with the rest of the world, with her membership of the United Nations, or with the awakened cosmopolitanism of many of her national leaders.

But on the face of it the U.S.A.'s immediate post-war conduct

gave ground for apprehension. There was her complete and precipitate disarmament, apart from atom bomb production and
research. There was her abrupt ending of Lend-Lease to Britain, a
grievous and unjust blow to the prospects of British recovery.

Lease-Lend had come to be more than an act of national generosity and foresight. By 1944–5 it had grown into an accepted and
planned division of the war burden. Great Britain had disposed of
a great part of her overseas assets, in meeting her war expenditure,
before the United States entered the conflict as an active belligerent.
Throughout the war Britain mobilized a greater proportion of her
resources for direct military action than any other nation engaged in
the war. For all practical purposes her export trade had been sacrificed to the immediate emergency.[32] Britain was able to act in this
way because of the assumption that the needs of her population
would be supplied under Lease-Lend. Thus what had begun as aid
was transformed into a division of labour. The original description
remained, but the character of the transaction had changed.

By the end of the war the economy of the United Kingdom was
inextricably interlocked with that of the United States. The cease-
fire could not change that situation at once. It is easy and most
pleasant to stop firing guns; but you cannot proceed to eat them.
The position of the United States was different. It was reasonable
to expect that a period should be allowed for the British economy
to adjust itself. This period was not vouchsafed her. The flow of
goods from the United States ceased at once, and what the United
Kingdom needed, she now had to buy, long before her mutilated
export trade could be rebuilt to meet the cost.

When the Labour government took over in 1945 this was the
situation it had to meet. I thought then, and I still think, that the
U.S.A. at that time imposed terms that were shortsighted and
unwarranted. It would be wholly wrong to describe this attitude as
British mendicancy. It is not mendicancy to expect that the immediate consequences of a wartime alliance should be mutually
shared just as the burden of war itself had been shared.[33] Later on
Marshall Aid repaired some of the damage; but in the meantime
fears of renewed American isolationism had grown.

Nor was this fear assuaged by the speeches of many prominent

Republicans. In the result it meant that British policy was bedevilled by the political situation in the United States. I know I shall be told that this is the price we have to pay for democratic processes. I reply at once that the main theme of this book is that concerted and sustained collective action is rendered impossible in nations whose policies are determined by pressure groups representing limited and often anti-social interests. If these pressure groups were acting in a vacuum it would not matter. But it does matter if the fate of mankind, of the United States, as well as other nations, is decided by interests which put their private plans and acquisitive desires before the obvious needs of the human race. The economic triumphs of the American system will avail the American people nothing in the absence of an overriding social conscience and social discipline.

When American foreign policy did concern itself with what was happening in the rest of the world, it did so out of fear – fear of Communism – fear of Communism in other parts of the world, and fear of how it would impinge itself, not only on the free institutions of the West, but also how it would affect what is described as the 'American way of life'.

Fear is a very bad adviser. Its companion is hate, and hate is the father and mother of cruelty and intolerance. Fear of Soviet Communism has led the United States, and those who follow her lead, to take a distorted view of the world situation, and of the forces which are at work in modern society. The reader who has been good enough to follow me thus far in this book will have gathered that I look upon free institutions as not only the most desirable of political systems, not only as the one most congenial to the flowering of human genius, but as indispensable in a modern industrial community. But these institutions are threatened not only by political dictatorships. The resistance to social and economic change that private and sectional interests are able to offer, thus undermining the faith of the masses in their regenerating power, can be equally deadly.

One question will serve to bring this out more clearly. Why is it that rearmament on the present scale meets with less resistance in the United States than it does anywhere else ? One answer will occur at once. The United States can better afford it. But that is my case. The people of Europe love liberty just as much as do the American people; and they are more immediately exposed to the peril of Soviet military aggression. If the armies of the Soviet orbit break out, the first victims will be in France, Italy, Belgium, Holland and Western Germany: after those, Great Britain. Why, in these circumstances, do the military advisers of the United States place, even on civil defence, more emphasis than do the nations of Europe, although America has greater physical immunity?

Or does the American administration think it understands the threat of Communism better than we do? Our view is that they understand it less and, in consequence, are feeding the peril of Communism as much as they are combating it. The United States is very strong, but is she sure she is as wise as she is strong? The weapons of the Soviet Union are in the first instance economic, social and ideological: only secondarily military. If Russia relied primarily upon military action why has she not resorted to it before now? The atom bomb is no answer. That is a constant factor. The Western powers have assured the Soviet Union of their present weakness and of their future strength. Why has Russia waited for the strength of the Western Powers to grow? Influential publicists in the United States are continually saying that they believe a showdown is inevitable. Why should Russia wait for a time most unfavourable to her? Winston Churchill recently stated in the House of Commons that he asked a well-informed diplomat when he thought war was most imminent and the diplomat replied 'last year'. But the rearmament of the Western powers is hardly under way at the moment of writing. Why has Russia not struck? These questions really must be faced.

Few will suggest that the Soviet Union would not seek a local military advantage. But it seems clear she would not wish to press it to the point of general conflagration. Some irresponsible advisers have suggested that this is a reason for us going all out in Manchuria. But that could precipitate a third world war; for Russia might then conclude that she had come to the end of the usefulness of her social and ideological weapons.

This is a time for frankness. Why do these arguments, which are obvious, have so little effect on most of the advisers of the American administration, or indeed, on European Conservatives, British included. For the simple reason that it is easier to frame a military reply to the Soviet threat than a social and economic one.

An effective answer to Russian aggression involves a re-examination of our attitude to the social problems in our own country. This may not be so urgent in the United States, where a buoyant economy still appears to give a rough satisfaction to the people of that country; nor in Britain where the success of the Labour government underpinned the democratic constitution. But it is otherwise in France, Italy and certainly in those parts of the world where hunger meets feudalism in head-on collision.

It is indeed a grim conclusion to which we are driven. The most valuable allies of the Soviet are those elements in society which fight against social reforms, for these would rather risk war than part with wealth and privilege on any great scale. We must face the inexorable logic of the situation. Free political institutions do not excite people to defend them with abandon, against the threat of another nation, if those institutions prove inadequate to protect their well-being at home. Liberal principles do not thrive without roots, and those roots are fed by the contentment, and therefore the love, of those who see in them the prospects of progressive amelioration.

It is because of these considerations that I believe the guidance given to the world by the United States administration is wrong. It has mistaken the nature of the menace, and so it not only prescribes the wrong remedy, but the remedy itself feeds the danger. The scale of rearmament urged upon the democracies by the United States is a source not of strength but of weakness. The recent resignations of British Ministers were occasioned by the belief that the speed and scale of rearmament demanded by the United States would increase world economic tensions to the point where the Soviet diplomatic offensive would be assisted. And so it has proved.

By the end of 1950, British recovery had reached the stage where it could dispense with Marshall Aid eighteen months before it was due to end. A substantial Budget surplus promised a long-awaited reward for the patient and industrious people of Britain. The central reserves were sufficient to increase confidence in the sterling area. This had been accomplished under a Socialist administration. At no time since the end of the 1914 war was the British Communist Party so weak. We had proved to all, except those too blinded by prejudice to be able to see, how democratic institutions could be used to hold back Communism, and solve the economic problems of the post-war world. And all that time, be it noted, Britain had been devoting a larger proportion of her national income to defence than the United States.[34]

One thing I must make clear. British Socialists were not preoccupied with Communism. What we did was not done to combat the fear of the Kremlin. We hardly gave it a thought. We simply went about the task of applying the principles we had been brought up to believe in, and they proved equal to the need. We were for, not anti. I am here speaking specifically of domestic issues.

In foreign affairs the ascendancy of the United States was all too painfully clear. She had emerged from the war with her economy stronger than when she entered it, a tribute not only to the vigour of her industry, but to her geographical position and to the role she had been allotted in the allocation of wartime tasks.

The dominating world position of the United States would have been much easier to accept if there had been a clear idea of what she wanted to do with it. To that there was no clue, except, of course, that she was against Communism. It was also obvious from many of the speeches of her principal spokesmen that she was almost as strongly opposed to British Socialism.

Here I must pay a tribute to many individual Americans closely associated with the American administration. They knew what was happening in Great Britain and they admired much of what they knew. But over and over again we were made aware of the obstacles they met at the hands of American big business. The achievements of the British government were consistently misrepresented. Anti-Socialist Americans listened to their opposite numbers in Britain. Above all they listened to Mr Winston Churchill, unable to appreciate that his defeat in 1945 made it impossible for him to assess accurately what was taking place. He was also handicapped by a marked illiteracy about all things economic. During the war this had been a tower of strength. He had only to throw the Union Jack over twenty tanks to see them as a hundred. Fortunately the enemy also saw them in the same light. But in peacetime, this impressionistic arithmetic worked in reverse. Twenty tractors produced by a Socialist government shrank to a minus quantity. Unfortunately the American public did not understand his subjective approach and accepted his jeremiads at their face value. Naturally many American business men were only too ready to believe that British Socialism was failing. They appear to be much more credulous about the success of Soviet industry.

Looking back over that period, I am still astonished at the way we were obsessed by the internal political situation in the United States. She always seemed to be going into an election, emerging from one, or in the throes of one. On each occasion Europe waited with bated breath for what would happen. By now we are accustomed to the uncertainties of the French political system. But there is one consolation about France. Her foreign policy is fairly consistent. It is otherwise with the United States, or at least it appears so.

I thought we were unduly apprehensive. It seemed to me it would have been better for us to take our line and stick to it, and let the United States react to us instead of us to her. I still think it would have been better for both of us – and for the rest of the world.

Up to the Korean incident American Far Eastern policy floundered from one extreme to another. At first she put all her money on the Chinese Nationalists. When these failed, she turned her back on the whole area, and gave it up as a bad job. Reports in responsible American newspapers made it clear that she would not give her support to our remaining in Hong Kong. Our position was simple. We are there by right of treaty. If China wishes to ask for a revision of the treaty we are ready to discuss it. But we would not be driven out by aggression. We reinforced our garrison in Hong Kong despite the American attitude.

From the beginning we believed that China was not anxious to sever all connexions with the Western world. We felt that she would not want to be wholly dependent on the Soviet Union. Hong Kong is her bridge with us as it is ours with her.

So far we have proved right and America wrong. It is still a matter for conjecture whether those who invaded South Korea did not think that the United States had disinterested herself in the Far East and that, therefore, it was safe for them to try their hand.

The United States reaction to early reverses in Korea was sharp, and, in my view, unbalanced. She was alarmed at what she considered the weakness of the Western powers in relation to the Soviet Union. To her mind there was nothing for it but an all-out rearmament drive to make good the deficiency. To a detached observer there was another angle. If Korea probed American weakness, it also revealed Russian strength. Yet Russia did nothing about it except to keep on helping North Korea. If American reasoning was correct, this was Russia's opportunity. Why didn't she take it?

Here we are back once more to the main argument. There is no evidence to show that the Soviet Union wants a trial of strength. She can, of course, fall into it. But it is easier for a dictatorship to pull out of such a situation than it is for a democracy. A dictatorship has no public opinion to satisfy.

The reaction of the United States to the revelation of her military unpreparedness for a major war dealt a deadly blow to Europe's hopes for economic recovery, and at the same time sent a cold wind throughout the backward regions of the world. It revealed the weakness of the motive behind President Truman's Point Four.[35] If this motive had been entirely altruistic it might have stood the strain. I have no doubt about his intentions: but unfortunately it had been represented to the American people as the bulwark against the spread of Communism. Korea raised the question: Have we time for Point Four to operate? At once the military experts said no!

I have already said that this is a time for frankness. There has never been any diffidence on the part of American public men in saying what they think about other people. I propose to follow their example. It astonishes the British people to witness the lattitude given to the Chiefs of Staff of the United States to air their views in public, not only about matters within their technical province, but also concerning the political assumptions behind national defence.

The right of military chiefs to conduct political propaganda is always dangerous to civilian government. This would concern only the people and government of the United States, were it not for the fact that we are all involved in the estimate of defence expenditure which is the direct result of the political atmosphere created by this propaganda.

Military experts have no easier task than to advise their government on the level of defence expenditure. All they have to do is to advise a larger sum than they know their government is prepared to concede and they are quite safe. In my experience this is invariably how they behave. If everything turns out satisfactorily, no questions are asked by a relieved public. If, on the other hand, disaster is encountered, the military expert is free from blame. The real burden of anxiety falls on the civilian Cabinet members who have to set the general needs of the national economy against the clamour of the military experts backed by a press always ready to capitalize on panic.

This is precisely what we have witnessed since the early months of the fighting in Korea. The military advisers demanded, and the governments of the West conceded, a level of rearmament, without paying the slightest attention to its effect on the economies of the nations concerned. This is proved, not only by the world inflation now raging, but by the fact that only now is a serious examination being made of the relative burdens to be borne by the nations of the North Atlantic Treaty Organization. We are all of us caught in the maelstrom created by panic estimates.

No one is less fitted than a military expert to weigh the economic consequences of his inordinate demands. Yet the nature of the modern military machine makes it more than ever necessary that the industrial repercussions should be carefully weighed, before heavy military expenditure is embarked upon. This was not done either in Britain or in the United States. In the latter it was perhaps not so important, because the national economy was not stretched by full employment as was the case in Britain. But even in the United States little regard appears to have been given to the effect on world prices of the uncontrolled spate of stockpiling which followed immediately on the announcement of the arms programme.

The arms programme, agreed on in the summer of 1950, was not sufficient to meet the needs regarded as militarily desirable. Before the year was out a still heavier programme was demanded; and all to be accomplished in three years, by which time, we were told, we could 'talk to Russia out of strength'. I have already pointed out that it seems insane for Russia to wait for that date, if her real intention is a military show-down. She is obviously less belligerent than some American publicists.

But why three years? What gives the year 1953 so portentous a significance? In no discussion have I heard the slightest justification for the date. It appears to bear the same relationship to scientific prediction as astrology has to astronomy. Does it mean that by that year it is believed Russia will be prepared and ready to move? But by that time even the more modest arms programme of the middle of 1950 would place her in a position of military inferiority. Or does it mean that by that time the Western powers will be prepared and determined to present an ultimatum to the Soviet Union? If so, this is a recipe for racial suicide.

It is necessary to examine this aspect of the question still further. It is expected that by the spring of 1953 the arms expenditure of the United States, including foreign aid, will reach the immense sum of sixty-five billion dollars or fifty per cent of the budget, and equal to eighteen per cent of the gross national product. By that time the arms programme will be the bully of the national economy. So far the history of the United States shows that it is her habit to arm for war and disarm for peace. The question now arises, can she arm for peace? The answer must depend to some extent on the arms burden she imposes on herself. If it proves too grievous, she will be impatient for some dramatic improvement in international relations. Experience shows this rarely happens. It is juvenile to suppose that today one feels insecure, and therefore arms, while tomorrow the fear disappears and one can relax. No such black-and-white changes can be expected. In such circumstances the temptation to precipitate action is obvious. It may well be that so great are the resources of the American economy that it can carry the arms burden without undue strain. But this is certainly not the case with her allies. Already, at the time of writing, France and Britain have been compelled to lower the living standards of their peoples, and it is hard to see how still further retrenchment can be avoided and still carry the arms programme.

The claim is now made that the United States should make a financial contribution to enable her Allies to meet their defence commitments. But that is to put the cart before the horse. One of two conclusions follows. Either the programme is too high, or the United States is not carrying her fair share of it. The clumsiest method, and the one most hurtful to national pride, is to make a direct contribution to help a nation finance its own defence. This has the appearance, if not the effect, of making the soldiers of European nations mercenaries of the United States State Department. It also undermines their independence in council. It is to the interest of none of us that our spokesmen should feel inhibited by the knowledge that their means of defence are at the mercy of one member of the Alliance. Nor should it be forgotten that speeches of Congressmen during appropriation debates are deeply wounding to the feelings of other nations, as these listen to their country's defence efforts, or policies, being discussed by the representatives of another nation. American Congressmen, like the rest of us, are entitled to decide how their money shall be spent, and for what. But they should be in a position to do so without running the risk of injuring the Alliance.

If a nation's share of the arms programme is insupportable, then the total should be lowered or the burden redistributed. Any other solution is inconsistent with dignity and national independence.

As I have said earlier, the duty of assessing the danger to peace, is ultimately one for the civilian authority. It is not a matter for soldiers. They are bound to play for the widest possible margin of safety. That is what they have done, and the result is a resounding diplomatic success for the Soviet Union.

In the present unbalanced condition of the world economy, an overassessment of Soviet military power is as dangerous as an underassessment. The former risks economic ruin. The latter invites military adventures. Soviet insistence on building up her war machine has alarmed the world. It is my contention that we have allowed her to alarm us into an irrational response. Some rearmament was forced upon us. Russian peace propaganda is a sham, and a cynical sham at that, as Vishinsky's behaviour at the United Nations Assembly in Paris revealed to all not blinded by fanaticism. I believe his sinister amusement was based on Russia's conviction that she had frightened the world into an arms race which will deepen economic tensions. It is upon the results of these tensions she finally relies for success, and only secondarily on her war machine. She knows that she has no chance of emerging victorious from a general conflict.

Each nation is conscious of its own weakness and of its enemies' strength. Up to a few years ago no high ranking soldier I talked to knew the figure of Russia's steel production. They had not bothered to find out. They based their defence estimates on what they knew Russia possessed in the way of actual weapons. Since every soldier thinks of the next war largely in terms of the last, they made their calculations in terms of a Russian blitzkrieg after the fashion of Hitler's early offensive in Western Europe. There is no evidence to show that Russia thinks in this way, nor would it be consistent with the nature of her economy, which is sluggish and resistive, not mobile and offensive. It would be expecting miracles of Russian industry if it were otherwise. A steel production of thirty million tons per year, only recently achieved – if she has even yet done so – servicing a population of more than two hundred millions, provides no basis for blitzkrieg methods of war.

Oh, I know I shall be told that she holds down the civil consumption of steel, and is able to devote a far larger proportion of it to war purposes than is the case with other nations. Even conceding that, the contrast with the steel production at the disposal of the Western powers is grotesque. The allies dispose of an annual steel production of 128 million tons and have a potential output of 180 million tons.[36]

There is no better test of the military striking power of a nation than its steel consumption. It represents not merely its ability to forge the weapons of modern war, but its capacity to replace and service them, along with the skills and know-how in the possession of thousands of technicians and craftsmen of all kinds. This the Russian rulers know probably better than we do, and it is this knowledge that will restrain their military adventures unless they are panicked into more than limited aggression.

No modern nation makes war unless she has no other way out, or unless she thinks she has a military organization which would give quick victory. This Hitler thought he possessed. There is no doubt that Russia has units organized in much the same way. She has the spearhead; but the shaft stretches too far back to the Urals to be wielded with swift precision.

Not only that, but such action on her part would lose her the support of those millions in Western Europe who still cherish the delusion that Russia yearns only for peace. No matter how the onslaught might be dressed up and presented as defence, the presence of Russian soldiers would bring about sharp disillusionment, and consolidate the populations of the invaded countries against her.

These considerations, among others, make the intervention of the United States in the affairs of Europe a matter of great delicacy. It would be fatal if European people were given the impression that they had to choose between two streams of intervention, Russian or American. This applies with even greater force to the Middle East where an insurgent nationalism is complicating a situation already sufficiently difficult.

An important part of the solution to these problems is to place increasing emphasis on the role of the United Nations and less on regional pacts, for these tend to wear the appearance of instruments of dominant powers. The effect of the Soviet-dominated bloc within the United Nations has been to stimulate the creation of a Western bloc and this tends to reduce the United Nations Assembly to the status of an arena in which the blocs manœuvre for position.

All this arises from a fundamental failure to appreciate the character of the present world revolution. This is taking a form which would lead to the defeat of Soviet diplomacy if its significance were properly grasped. Soviet expansionist aims have already received a sharp setback, for though uprisings of the colonial peoples, and the revolution in the Orient, are applauded and given limited aid, they are at best viewed with mixed feelings. It was not

F

there that Soviet Russia hoped for her greatest successes. She had reckoned on achieving these among the urban populations of the advanced industrial countries. Nor was this expectation without historical foundation. The philosophy applied to Russia after the 1914–1918 war was a product of the Industrial Revolution. It was born in London, Berlin, Paris and New York: not in Rostov, Kiev and Leningrad.

As I have already sought to make clear, the leaders of the Soviet Revolution were conditioned from the outset by the necessity to extract surpluses from a backward agrarian population. This led them to adopt practices that brought about a progressive distortion of their óriginal principles. It is this distortion the industrial masses of the West are unwilling to accept. Political helotry is not a condition congenial to the psychology of an artisan population.

The history of the last thirty years would have been different if the advanced industrial techniques of the West could have been joined to the agrarian hinterland of Russia. But it was not to be, and in the meantime the original impetus of the Russian Revolution was polluted and maimed beyond recognition.

It gives little satisfaction to the Soviet rulers to know that contemporary revolutions are occurring in the same kind of milieu. If you amalgamate a Russian peasant with a Chinese peasant you don't make a steelworks. The remorseless logic of this is apparent in Peking no less than in Moscow. Unfortunately it does not seem to impress Washington in the same degree. A wise and far-seeing statesmanship would grasp this central fact, and make it the basis of policy. China is not the natural ally of Russia. It is not enough, in reply, to say that the leaders of the Chinese People's Government were trained in Moscow and that they use the terminology of Soviet Communism. It would be much more astonishing if they used the language of Colonel McCormick.

The outstanding need of China, as of similar communities, is for the industrial products of the urban communities of the West. These Russia is not able to supply in anything approaching the quantities required. Indeed, just to the extent that Russia has perverted her own economy to war purposes, she is unable to assist in supplying the civilian requirements of her temporary allies.

It is a grim commentary on the direction taken by the Russian revolution that the North Koreans found it easier to obtain tanks than tractor ploughs from their Soviet 'friends'.

But is not the West making just that same mistake? We have allowed the Russian threat to divert us from the one policy that might help to pacify the world. The answer to social upheaval is social amelioration, not bombing planes and guns; yet we are making the latter on such a scale that we have no resources left for the provision of the industrial equipment which the under-developed areas of the world must have if they are not to go on bubbling and exploding for the rest of the century.

The amount set aside for Point Four purposes has been reduced to derisory proportions and even then it is subordinated to military considerations. It is a profound mistake to look upon our relations with backward peoples simply as one aspect of the struggle with the Soviet Union. If the Soviet system did not exist, the problem would still be there.

In the United States, in Britain, and to some extent in most European countries, the relations between industry and the countryside are more balanced than has ever before been the case in the history of the human race. We are well on the way to solving the problem that brought down the civilizations of antiquity. Urban life does not flourish against a background of intolerable rural exploitation. Much has still to be done. The countryside, especially the deep countryside, lacks many of the amenities enjoyed by the urban areas. But the disparity decreases. One further push and we can make the advantages and disadvantages of town versus country labour roughly comparable. But this applies only to a small minority of the people of the world. It is not true of India, Pakistan, Burma, Siam, China, the Middle East and large parts of Africa, including Egypt.

If this situation made demands only on our capacity to sympathize with the distress of others, its urgency would be in direct ratio to our standards of civilized behaviour. But even the most unimaginative among us should be able to see that there is more to it than that. Our own lives are deeply involved and commingled with the lives of the people living in the backward parts of the world.

The needs of our industries have brought them into our back yard. They now bear the same relationship to the urban communities of the West as the rural peoples of ancient times bore to the thin urban fringe in which civilization flourished for a time, and then was extinguished by the flood from the hinterland.

The advanced industrial communities of the West can make little more progress, they cannot even stabilize themselves, without sharing the achievements of their industries and sciences with the rest of the world. Even opulent and almost self-sufficient North America is becoming aware of this. On Monday, 12 November, 1951, the *New York Times* printed an editorial in the course of which it said: '. . . Obviously we are going to become more and more dependent upon foreign raw materials in the field of metals and upon increasingly low quality domestic ores . . . To the extent that we are increasingly dependent upon foreign sources, we are coming to be increasingly vulnerable to interruptions in supply consequent upon political developments or in wartime interruptions of shipping . . . Here is a set of fundamental problems which is already bedevilling this generation and will perturb our children and their children even more. It is to be hoped our policy-makers realize the full gravity of these questions and are not losing sight of them as they strive to solve the more immediately urgent short deficits impinging on our economy today.'

One obvious lesson the *New York Times* failed to draw from its own analysis, is that the prudent use of scarce resources cannot be expected from a *laissez-faire* economy. Private economic adventure will continue to burn up the dwindling supplies of precious metals with the same regardlessness for the future, as was formerly shown by the destruction of forest lands and the riches of the surface soils. Capitalism builds up its own capital at the expense of the exhaustible capital existing in nature; and calls its myopic prodigality the success of private enterprise. It is easier to construct a conveyor belt than it is to replace the raw materials consumed by it. Solar energy is the nearest approach to a conveyor belt nature shows us, but we have not yet learned to reconstruct its components into the materials for our industries, even though we may in time harness its energy as driving power.

Point Four projects are therefore matters of substance and urgency for all of us. It is not enough to see the problem. It must be tackled and all its implications faced even if this involves painful heartsearching and the dawning of wonderment as to whether the Western way of life really has the permanence so often claimed for it.

In the meantime, rearmament intensifies the problem by consuming ever-increasing quantities of just those materials that are running ominously short. We have already been warned by geologists, and mineralogists that the consumption of another world war might well ruin us from this cause alone, apart from all the other grim consequences.

Elsewhere in this book I discuss the need for a reputable order of values in modern society if we are to deserve the name civilization. It is pertinent at this point to mention one of them. If it be the case – and it is by now, I should have thought, irrefutable – that most, if not all, the peoples of the world are linked together in an endless variety of reciprocal activities, then the condition of each one of us becomes the concern of all of us. This is only the ethical formulation of an irrefragable fact. In these circumstances, we neglect at our peril its many implications. The Great Societies of the West draw many of the materials for their way of life from parts of the world where millions suffer actual hunger and are ravaged by diseases which are the direct result of malnutrition. This is not only manifestly unjust. It is also exceedingly unsafe for us. We are witnessing some of the consequences in Persia and Egypt. In the words of the *New York Times*, we are dependent on the 'political developments' of the countries concerned. One of these 'developments' is resentment against appallingly bad social conditions suffered by the masses in these lands, even as they see wealth taken from their country to add to the wealth of people already enjoying standards of living spectacularly higher than their own. If these people were our own countrymen, we should long ago have remedied their worst distresses. Yet they are our countrymen in the sense that our industry is interlocked with theirs.

One of the main answers of the Western allies to this situation is the creation of a Middle East Defence Pact. The underfed masses yearn for material aid; we send them guns. This is the answer of the soldier to a problem he ought not to be asked to solve. If asked, he gives the only reply within his competence.

Once these pacts are made, military needs require order and stability in the countries forming them. The social and political ambitions of the masses, in these circumstances, are seen as opposed to our military necessities, and before we know where we are our armed forces are enlisted on the side of the oppressors in those countries. It is an ugly and lamentable situation, and it all arises from trying to solve the wrong problem. The problem is primarily social and economic, not military and strategic.

The political systems of the totalitarian nations might remain fixed for an indefinite time, if they could prevent the intrusion of modern industrial methods. But they are reaching out for these, and to the extent that they adopt them, they start the same chain of events that led to the growth of political democracy in the West. The only political system consistent with the needs of a modern industrial community is democracy. It is not possible to educate workers to perform the thousand and one activities necessary to modern industry and still expect them to tolerate political subservience. When you train workers to make the blueprints of modern industrial machines, to interpret the blueprints, make and work the machines, you are digging the grave of political dictatorship.

It is no answer to point to Nazi Germany. For ten short years she tried to violate the laws of modern society. As a result she produced a society barbarous, perverted, and bloody, and it ended in a collapse as complete as any in history. Hitler could make his dictatorship of a technically highly-trained people near tolerable only by a social extroversion so monstrous that it produced a national psychology of a morbidity that still fascinates students of social psychology.

It takes time for industrialization to influence the political aspirations of a people, and it takes longer in some countries than in others. Where democracy has never existed it takes a long time for the ferment to work. In the Soviet Union, for instance, it must be accepted that the vast mass of workers are conscious of emancipation and not of slavery. When the Soviet worker of today compares his lot with that of his parents, he is aware of enlargement, and not of constriction. He is now literate. They could neither read nor write. Many occupations are open to him where they were confined to the narrow frontiers of the village and the repetitious cycle of a primitive agriculture. For him the barriers are down. He can become a mechanic, a teacher, a doctor, an artist, a professor, or a foreman or manager in a large industrial undertaking. It is completely unhistorical to expect him to take any other view than that Soviet society has lifted him to higher levels of opportunity and culture. The picture of the Russian worker held down by a ruthless dictatorship is false. He is indoctrinated by a consistent propaganda which tells him that the workers of the capitalist world are infinitely worse off than he is, and the lack of communication with the rest of the world fosters this delusion. But his support of the Soviet regime does not rest even partly on this. It rests on his own knowledge that all around him the framework of a modern industrial community is being built, that he is helping to build it, and that in the meantime his life is substantially, if slowly, improving.

This is not an apologia for the Soviet regime. We all know there are features of the Soviet system which are repulsive. The existence of huge forced labour camps, the ruthless punishment meted out to political offenders, the disappearance without trace of people who offend against the ruling clique, the appalling doctrine of 'associative crime'; all these are deeply offensive. But I should say only an insignificant minority of the Russian people are aware of them. In that vast country, and among a population of more than 200 million, many things can occur unknown to most of the people. It is astonishing how many Germans were unaware of the monstrosities committed by the Nazis. The apparatus of a modern dictatorship is terrible, not only in what it does, but in its ability to do it clandestinely.

It is necessary that we keep all these things in their proper historical perspective if we are to avoid a black-and-white view of the world. Mankind is not born with an insatiable appetite for political liberty. This is the coping stone on the structure of progress, not its base. If political liberty and the institutions which enshrine it were the spontaneous imperatives of the human spirit, our task would be much easier. But they are earth-bound and time-bound. The pulse of progress beats differently for different parts of the world, and if we are to understand what is happening around us and act intelligently about it, we must recognize that fact and realize that once we stood where they now stand.

And it is just because we have passed that way ourselves that we should be optimistic about the future. Industrialization is lifting increasing numbers of Russians to technical and economic importance in the Soviet economy. Their economic enfranchisement is proceeding. Political enfranchisement must follow. Economic importance combined with political nullity cannot last. They never have yet, and there is no reason to suppose the Soviet system will be any different. The desperate attempts made by the Soviet rulers to insulate themselves from the rest of the world is proof of this. It is not merely that they want to conceal from Russians the higher standards of living elsewhere. That is true, but there is more to it than that. They don't want their technicians and their professional and managerial classes to become too familiar with the higher political status enjoyed by their opposite numbers in other countries. Political freedom and the social status that goes with it is a heady wine once sipped. The controversies which raged recently in Soviet academic and artistic circles show how fertile the social soil is becoming. It is the topmost branches of the tree that first reveal the rising breeze.

There is evidence also that the Soviet government wishes to disengage itself from Eastern Germany. In going so far West the Soviet Union pushed itself beyond its sociological frontiers. Its monolithic system of government and administration are proving ill-adapted to digest the more variegated texture of Western life. It is not as easy to force centralism upon administrators accustomed to administrative initiative as upon those who have known nothing else.

Poland, Czechoslovakia, Hungary and Eastern Germany are not only satellites. They are also fringe states where the over-simplified edicts of Soviet centralist policy cause endless irritation. There is little hope that the satellites will break away from Soviet domination. They are too tightly held for that. The peril to Soviet authority is more subtle. The complicated industrial system of the satellite states and the commerce attending upon it impose local responsibilities which have to be undertaken by individuals who stand or fall by the decisions they take. The independence of mind resulting from that situation provokes countless points of resistance, and each point is a focus of dissatisfaction.

For the present, it would be unreasonable to expect any overt expression of discontent in the masses of the Soviet Union. The individual Soviet citizen does not wish to break down his social framework, because it still affords him scope for the extension of his personality. Until his wants have grown to the point where he is conscious of constriction he will not protest.

What form that protest will take when it comes is difficult to conjecture. The machinery of oppression in a modern dictatorship is powerful and universal. The whole history of mankind contains no parallel. So dependent is the modern large-scale community on communication, that any group within it, when denied its use, is paralysed. Its individual members are atomized. They know only one collectivity and that is the one permitted by the regime. There is therefore no spontaneous generation of an alternative to the existing government. So far man has invented only three methods of transmitting political power from one generation to another: dynastic, caste and property. Not one of the three exists among the modern dictatorships. There are some who say they discern the beginnings of caste in the one-party system, but this I doubt. This was possible in a comparatively primitive community where most of the important functions of group life could be discharged by relatively few persons. This is not the case in an industrialized country. There, power is ultimately shared with those whose economic co-operation must be ensured. These eventually comprise all the workers, for the creation, maintenance and expansion of modern industrial techniques depend upon a literate and trained population.

This is a problem the Soviet states have not yet faced. A succession of purges takes the place of replacement by free elections. The principle of authority has replaced the authority of principle which inspired the Revolution in the first instance. Government by

F *

authority dominated the history of man until the universal
franchise and representative institutions established themselves
in the Western world in the late nineteenth and early twentieth
centuries.

In the meantime our job is to find a positive way of lightening
economic pressures and easing world tensions. These are worsened
and not helped by the scale and pace of rearmament and by regional
pacts aimed at containment and the status quo. It is as though we
expect the world to be stationary while we engage in complicated
strategical manœuvres. The essence of genius, it has been said, is
to align oneself with the inevitable. This is as true today as it was
when emergent America rejected the ridiculous pretensions of
George III.

Revolutions are now taking place in nations which have lain
dormant for thousands of years. Our task is to accommodate them
within a general pattern of world co-operation. World leadership
must take account of world movements or it condemns itself to
futility. For a long time to come we shall be living in an apprehensive and unsafe world, so the means of collective discipline must
be available. But that must not be allowed to deflect us from a
purposive and sustained attack on the long-term causes of disturbance.

Judged from this attitude, the refusal to admit the new China
into the United Nations and the continued recognition of the
Chiang Kai-shek regime is peevish and unrealistic. It may be hard
for the moment to do the former, while Chinese troops are killing
the soldiers of the United Nations, but it is better to have China
unrepresented in the meantime than to have its place filled by
people who represent nothing but a rump, and whose very presence
threatens the Chinese people with a renewal of the civil war from
which they have suffered for so many years.

With the defeat of aggression in Korea and the consequent
assertion of the authority of the United Nations, the time will
come for a reconsideration of the status of Formosa. It is impossible
to justify a refusal to cede it to China. Its eventual assimilation in
the Chinese People's Republic is an essential condition for the
pacification of the Far East.

The signing of the Japanese peace treaty, without the signature and agreement of the real government of China, was an extraordinarily flat-footed piece of diplomacy. It is difficult to see what long-term policy lay behind it unless it is one that certainly would not commend itself to European opinion. This is not world leadership. It is just querulousness, where it is not worse.

Against the background of mounting tension created by such policies, it is idle to talk of general disarmament. People are not, and never have been, prepared to throw their guns away while they feel unsafe. The guns are there because the sense of insecurity is there, not the insecurity because the guns are there. The existence of huge armaments directly contributes to the universal fear, but it is secondary, not primary. This applies as much to atom weapons as to more primitive types. Over-armament can multiply the tensions, economic and otherwise, as I have argued, but disarmament as a deliberate act must follow from a belief that co-operation in common tasks is possible; and that from that co-operation a general pacification will ensue, and this in its turn permit of agreement about arms.

Judged from this angle, interminable discussions at the United Nations about this or that disarmament proposal take on the appearance of cynical manœuvres calculated not to solve the problem, but merely to shift blame for the resultant deadlock from one side to the other.

Nor is it wise to concentrate all the time on the immediate causes of tension. All that this produces is an eager desire on the part of each contestant to think up as many differences as possible against the others. It certainly produces polemics. But it does not promote peace.

We should try to avoid new causes of tension, such as the re-arming of Western Germany. But it is reasonable to expect the old causes of tension to relax only after an experience of common endeavour.

At this stage it is not possible to put forward some novel proposal that will command immediate and universal commendation. The field of international relations has been too well explored, and by too many ingenious minds, to expect some inspired flash of

illumination to light up the way ahead for us. We shall reach the
destination we all seek at the end of a number of prosaic endeavours,
patiently pursued, and accompanied by setbacks and bitter
disappointments.

Whatever we decide upon must command the resources of
idealism if we are to surmount the fears and limited ambitions in
which international relations are now snarled. Nothing nearer than
a distant horizon will beckon us from where we are now bogged.
The instrument for the task cannot be one nation, nor a limited
combination of nations. It must be the Assembly of the United
Nations itself. Otherwise we shall start off in a climate of mutual
suspicion.

Nor is our goal the defeat of Communism, or of Socialism, or
the preservation of this or that way of life. It is not even the conquest of poverty, for that term is capable of so many different and
contradictory definitions. It is more limited than that. It is the
defeat of hunger in the most literal physical sense. Until hunger
has been left behind as a racial memory, it will not be possible to
say that man has won the decisive victory in his long struggle with
his physical environment. If hunger continues to be the lot of
millions of our fellow creatures, our civilization will not be safe
from the fate that overwhelmed previous civilizations.

Here we approach the core of one of our main fears. Will it one
day be found possible to halt the arms programme and begin
to divert economic resources to Point Four ends? This is a question addressed primarily to the United States of America, as it is
principally from her that substantial wealth can be made available
for world mutual aid. It will be a profound test of American
statesmanship.

If she remains convinced that the chief danger to peace is the
military aggressiveness of the Soviet bloc, then elements in the
American nation will want a showdown with the Russians, and the
danger of war will be immediately upon us. Negotiation by ultimatum is the shortest road to war. In such an atmosphere, economic
and financial pressures can be relied upon to worsen the diplomatic
situation; for so much wealth is tied up in the war machine, that
fears of universal deflation and consequent bankruptcies and

unemployment will thrust us either into military action or the continuation of arms production on a self-defeating scale.

The North American political system has not yet reached the point where it can digest its economic surpluses within its own economy. One American commentator, Mr James Warburg (*Victory without War*, p. 48), has described this surplus as six to seven billion dollars of 'hot money' – 'money which must be got rid of in one way or another if our economy is not to go into a tail-spin. At present we are getting rid of our "hot money" through rearmament. Without rearmament, we shall have to increase both our imports and our foreign investments. We cannot increase our imports – even with a sensible tariff – by more than perhaps two billion dollars, unless we continue stock-piling strategic materials. We must, therefore, plan as a normal peace-time procedure, the annual investment of four or five billion dollars abroad. Some of this will be private investment; eventually most of it should be private investment, once the world gets on an even keel. For the immediate future, we must contemplate public investment abroad on a large scale immediately our military expenditures are reduced. Our economy is unhealthy, primarily because we have never really adjusted it to our position as the world's largest creditor nation.'

Mr Warburg calls for action of the kind described on the morrow of peace. I take the view that such action is the condition of peace. A curtailment of the arms programme is essential to the release of wealth for Point Four purposes. The prime question is: will America ever feel safe enough to embark on such a programme in a period of international tension?

What is now required is that a reduction of arms expenditure should not be seen as the precursor of an industrial crisis. Otherwise fear of the effect of the industrial surplus will feed belligerency.

Long before the arms programme reaches its peak, realistic international discussions should take place for the substitution of an ambitious plan of world development to replace a substantial proportion of the expenditure on arms. This would give industry some protection against the dangers of a sharp deflation. The Soviet Union should be invited to take part in these discussions as a potential contributor. Since she spends so much of her resources on weapons of war, she too should be able to set something aside for help to backward areas; and the fact that the Western powers were ready to take these steps ought to go far to convince her that no aggressive military action is intended against her.

There will no doubt be many who can see no hope of success for any such project. Let me try to encourage them by an illustration from recent history.

When the Labour government took office in Britain in 1945, relations between India and Britain had degenerated to the point where they looked hopeless. It was useless for Britain to promise India eventual self-government. So many promises had been made that it had not been convenient to keep, that Indian opinion had moved from distrust to open hostility. The resources of statesmanship were apparently exhausted. Every attempt at negotiation by Britain looked to India as merely a device to postpone Indian sovereignty. Distrust frustrated negotiation and negotiation was unable to remove distrust.

And then the Labour Cabinet had an inspiration. Like all great decisions it was in essence simple. It consisted in fixing a definite date for the ending of British power in India and Pakistan. The date determined upon was far enough away to give time for discussions about the conditions of transfer. It was near enough to dissolve any doubt as to the sincerity of British intentions. At once a catalytic element was introduced into Anglo-Indian relations to which all else had to react. The day of liberation became a goal, a challenge, and an aspiration. Hostility melted away, and now warm friendship has taken the place of the accumulated bitterness of centuries.

The problem for mankind is how to get world opinion focused on something which is not the present hopeless contemplation of the drift to war. Is it possible to find here also a catalyst which will rivet the attention of the world on constructive tasks and optimistic ends? The generals have given us the dates of despair – 1952–3. Suppose we fix a date – towards which we should at once begin to work – when a definite percentage of what we are now spending on arms shall be set aside for the peaceful development of backward parts of the world. There are three essentials for success. The date should be far enough away for preparations to be made. It should be near enough to excite hope and encourage restraint. And the percentage of the arms programme proposed to be diverted to peaceful purposes should be definite, substantial, and capable of being expressed in terms of men and machinery.

If this were done, the extent of our movement away from the catastrophe towards which we are now heading could be measured in the increasing proportion of our resources diverted from war expenditure to peaceful development. Should the Soviet Union find it possible to co-operate, it would help partly to solve the vexed question of inspection that has proved such a stumbling block to disarmament. A contribution from the Russians to the peace plan would at once begin to restrict Soviet consumption of arms. It may be argued that she could accomplish this by reducing civil consumption. But we shall get nowhere by endless suspicion.

There is nothing complicated about this proposal. It should prove easier to work out in detail than some of the military plans now dominating the attention of statesmen. It would guarantee the absorption of economic surpluses where these threaten the livelihood of millions of workpeople. It would mobilize the energies and idealism of men and women everywhere. Optimism and buoyancy would begin to take the place of leaden despair.

Positive and constructive effort of this kind, with its resulting co-operation, would be worth scores of conferences on disarmament.

NOTE 32

It is not generally known that Britain lost approximately one quarter of her national wealth in the course of World War II. A rough estimate, at 1945 prices, of Britain's pre-war wealth, puts the figure at £30,000 million. According to *Statistical Material Presented During the Washington Negotiations* (Cmd. 6707, published by H.M.S.O. in December 1945, price 3*d*), we lost a total of £7,248,000,000, made up as follows:

Financial Losses.

Sales or repatriation of overseas investments	£1,118 mill.
Increase in sterling balances and overseas loans	2,928 ,,
Depletion of gold and U.S. dollar reserves	152 ,,
	£4,198 mill.

Physical Losses.

Destruction and damage to property	£1,450 mill.
Shipping losses	700 ,,
Depreciation and obsolescence not made good during the war period	900 ,,
	£3,050 ,,
Total	£7,248 ,,

In addition we had sacrificed two-thirds of our export trade. Our economy was distorted from top to bottom to enable the maximum war effort to be made. In mid-1945 the number of people serving in the armed forces and civil defence and employed in war industries totalled over 9 million, compared with 2 million in 1939. The national debt had increased from £7,130 million in 1939 to the staggering total of £21,366 million in 1945.

NOTE 33

Neither does the aid that Britain has received from the United States justify, as Conservative politicians are so fond of seeking to justify, the charge that Britain has played the beggar in international economic affairs. From the end of the war until mid-1950, Britain had received aid totalling £1,893 million. But during the same period, and despite her wartime losses, she had provided £1,570 million. The detailed figures are as follows:

Receipts by the United Kingdom to 30 June, 1950

U.S. and Canadian loans	£1,227 mill.
ERP loans and grants	667 ,,

Australian and New Zealand gifts	46 mill.
Drawing rights exercised under the Intra-European Payment scheme	18 „
Other capital transactions (International Monetary Fund drawings; *less* subscriptions, *less* repayments of loans)	—65 mill.
	£1,893 mill.

Payments by the United Kingdom to 30 June, 1950

Gifts	400 „
Loans	493 „
Drawing rights exercised under Intra-European Payments scheme	85 „
Reductions in sterling balances	319 „
Other capital transactions (investments *less* sales and redemptions)	273 „
	£1,570 mill.

NOTE 34

The 1950 *Report* of the Bank for International Settlements, as quoted by *The Economist* of 29 July, 1950, gives the actual percentages of defence expenditures in 1949 or 1949/50 incurred by various countries, in relation to their respective national incomes:

	Percentage		*Percentage*
United Kingdom	7.4	Sweden	3.6
Netherlands	6.1	Canada	3.0
United States	5.9	Switzerland	2.7
Turkey	5.8	Belgium	2.5
France	5.0	Norway	2.5
Italy	3.8	Denmark	1.9

The *Economist* continues:

'The addition of 10 billion dollars a year to the defence expenditure of the United States will bring the percentage to almost exactly 10 per cent. The British figure is certainly going to rise to over 9 per cent, and these statistical comparisons are not accurate enough to be pressed within a closer margin than 1 per cent. For all practical purposes it is true to say that the British defence effort, which ever since the end of the war has been the highest, relative to the national resources, of any of the free nations, will stand comparison, as measured by expenditure, even with the new scale of American preparations.'

NOTE 35

The section of President Truman's inaugural address to Congress in January 1949 which put forward the proposal that the United States should co-operate in the economic and technical development of the backward areas is now popularly referred to as the 'Point Four' programme.

NOTE 36

According to the *Monthly Bulletin of Statistics* of the United Nations (September 1951) the steel-producing countries among the free nations of the world averaged the following monthly production of crude steel in 1950:

Australia	101,000 metric tons per month	
Belgium	314,000 ,, ,, ,, ,,	
Canada	256,000 ,, ,, ,, ,,	
France (including the Saar)	879,000 ,, ,, ,, ,,	
Italy	197,000 ,, ,, ,, ,,	
Luxemburg	204,000 ,, ,, ,, ,,	
Turkey	7,600 ,, ,, ,, ,,	
United Kingdom	1,380,000 ,, ,, ,, ,,	
United States	7,310,000 ,, ,, ,, ,,	
Giving a total of	10,648,600 ,, ,, ,, ,,	

Or an annual figure (for 1950) of 127,783,200 *metric tons.*
Western Germany, excluded from the above table, produced 1,010,000 tons per month during 1950, equivalent to an annual figure of 12,120,000 tons.

9

Raw Materials, Scarcities and Priorities

In earlier chapters I have frequently referred to the absence of any ordered system of priorities in what I have called, using the language of Graham Wallas, the Great Society. By priorities I mean the recognition by the community of first claims on its resources, which implies the acceptance of a hierarchy of moral values, not only in the governance of our private conduct but in that of the state as a whole.

Of course there are the traditional priorities, such as the judiciary, national defence and the police force; and as the Great Society expanded and became more complex, certain primitive disciplines were reluctantly accepted in the interests of public health and education, and in response to the repugnance evoked by the grosser consequences of neglect and personal ill-fortune. All these mitigated, even if they did not entirely remove, the results of stripping the communal authority of almost all but the most rudimentary functions and leaving the individual to fend for himself.

During the last fifty years or so all kinds of institutions and organizations have arisen to protect the individual against the rigours of unrestricted competition. The trade unions are a typical example of this. At first they were fiercely resisted and regarded as a prime offence against the gods of economic individualism.

Professional organizations also came into existence, though these often had a double intention, one to protect the interests of the members and the other to guarantee to the community standards of professional performance. Each new arrival modified the gaunt austerity of *laissez-faire* principles. Thus the citizen in the modern industrial society finds himself involved in a complex variety of involuntary obligations. Most of these are attempts to win some measure of control over a social environment in which the individual finds himself exposed to intolerable uncertainties and privations.

Just as society itself is a means of waging the struggle for survival in physical nature, so these various forms of collective action are mechanisms evolved to enable the individual to struggle successfully with his social environment. Neither in nature nor in society are we prepared to abandon the attempt at environmental control.

This is part of the answer to those who continue to swear by the virtues of private enterprise and universal competition. When we are told that these correspond with the basic impulses of 'human nature' we reply that the facts of human behaviour contradict this contention at every turn. Human nature is as much co-operative as it is competitive. Indeed, the complicated texture of modern society emphasizes over and over again the greater survival value of collective action.

Thus the grand priority that subordinated almost everything to individual success has come to be insensibly qualified by our obligations to the associations of which we are members, occupational and otherwise. But in spite of all this, 'official' thinking still persists in regarding the principles of economic individualism as characteristic of modern man in modern society. This attitude prevents us from facing the most important task of our generation, that is, making an evaluation of where we have reached and where we want to go from here: in short, working out a system of social priorities.

The climate of opinion in capitalist society is wholly opposed to this exercise. Nor should this occasion surprise. It is one of the tragedies of history that the application of social purposes or priorities, or whatever you like to call them, first occurred in economically backward countries. It has therefore been accompanied by excesses that have produced a revulsion against further experiments in the same direction. But this will not do. No amount of clamour against 'statism', no refusal to assess the historical significance of Soviet Communism in the modern world, and of the different kinds of Communism confused with it, nor yet the lumping together of all forms of purposeful political endeavour as an attempt to achieve the 'police state', can serve to conceal the central fact of our day. This is that a number of central aims must be worked out as guiding principles for our social and political activities, and to these all else must be related.

I do not attempt to belittle either the difficulty or the magnitude of the task. Free men using free institutions have never tried this before in the long history of mankind. But that should not frighten us. History is never a guide to contemporary action. And this for the very good and simple reason that the panorama of the centuries is not the unfolding of repetitious events. Each social circumstance is new not only in itself but in our disposition towards it. We must not allow ourselves to be deterred from the effort to introduce rational principles into social relations simply because it has never been done before – tradition, habit and authority having been made to suffice.

It is no accident that interest in the social sciences is a comparatively recent phenomenon. The coming into existence of the vast social aggregations of the modern world, thrown as they are into a continual ferment by the discoveries of the physical sciences, challenges the modern intellect just as the discovery of the New World excited the curiosity of our immediate forebears. Nor will the effort to organize society in accordance with rational principles be prevented by witch hunts and by the political proscriptions which disgrace the name of some countries at the present time.

It is true that intelligent collective conduct can be postponed by such behaviour, but what social advantage is there in that? The problem is simply made more difficult. Children are taught in our schools to respect Giordano Bruno and Galileo and other martyrs of science, and at the same time they are encouraged to close their minds against those who question the assumptions underlying contemporary society. Revolution is almost always reform postponed too long. A civilized society is one that can assimilate radical reforms while maintaining its essential stability. The real enemies of society are those who use popular slogans to deflect the attention of the masses from an objective study of the social and political issues of the day. That so many people suffer from preventable privation, while others enjoy privileges and material advantages that do not on any reasonable reckoning flow from personal accomplishments, is evidence of dangerous social instability. In modern conditions the acceptance of central social purposes has become a condition of man's survival: social morality and further progress are inextricably bound up, one with the other.

Nothing illustrates this more clearly than the contemporary attitude to mass unemployment. It is not necessary here to dwell on the consequences of unemployment for the unemployed themselves. These are well known and have been exhaustively expounded. But what have not been examined sufficiently are the implications of the determination to prevent unemployment from occurring. Some economists insist that the absence of a pool of idle labour means that it may not be possible to find labour for vital jobs. From this they proceed to argue that full employment has its corollary in the direction of labour, in short, that the attainment of the social aim of full employment implies industrial conscription. It is one of the curious features of the psychology of these gentlemen that they invariably contend that any general social good must always be at the expense of the working classes. But that is not the issue I wish to discuss here. What is more important is the consequence of making the pursuit of full employment a general social aim.

In a previous chapter it was pointed out that the maintenance of full employment always carries with it the threat of inflation, and that to avoid inflation there must be sustained control by the state of the investment programme. But even more than that is required. If all the factors of production, including labour, are in full use and something additional is required, that can be provided only at the expense of some already existing article of consumption. (I am assuming here no increase in productivity.) That means selection between different forms of consumption and that, in its turn, means arranging consumption in an order of priority. Once this is accepted, bang goes at once a whole series of fetishes of the competitive society. Consumer choice, for example, is no longer king of the market, nor is our old friend the so-called law of supply and demand, nor is the rate of profit any longer the sole arbiter of the employment of capital. Once the competitive society is compelled to serve a general social aim the automatism of the market is interfered with at every point and we are no longer in the capitalist system at all. We shall have abandoned selection by competition for selection by deliberation. From this point on, moral considerations take precedence over economic motives; and this because the choice between the worthwhileness of different forms of consumption implies an order of values. The decision what to do without, or take less of, necessarily places that particular item of consumption lowest in the order of priority.

This can best be seen at the present time in the impact of rearmament on the Western world. It has been accepted, rightly or wrongly – for the purpose of the argument it is no matter which – that our economic effort shall be subordinate to a general aim, the making of arms. In an economy already at full stretch this means the displacement of other kinds of production and therefore of consumption. What these shall be is now the issue of politics in the Western world. It is no longer decided only in the market place, in the financial houses, and by the price mechanism. No one questions the price of a tank. That is looked upon apparently as a general good; but a public health service is not – at least many do not think so.

In the case of defence requirements, fear of failure invokes the necessary social disciplines in the economic system, although even here the pursuit of profit frequently runs counter to the general will.

It must now be accepted by all thoughtful citizens that the social and economic consequence of the rearmament programme is only a special instance of a general case. If full employment is accepted as an aim to be followed, and not only given lip-service, then we have left the automatism of the competitive capitalist system behind us, and deliberate selection and choice at the communal level must take its place. A pool of unemployment is the necessary accompaniment of selection by the price mechanism. It is the shock absorber of the capitalist system. The pool decreases or increases in obedience to the ebb and flow of economic activity, and the unemployed are crucified on the cross of the competitive price mechanism. Security of employment and the competitive society are a contradiction in terms. To promise full employment is to promise the transition from the capitalist system to one where we choose consciously to order the pattern of production and consumption; the principles we employ in the doing of this must commend themselves to the wishes of a free electorate.

This dilemma has been recognized by many who are loath to accept its logic and therefore suggest an ingenious solution: what they call 'frictional unemployment'. By this is meant just enough unemployment to cause a pinch but not enough to make a wound. This, so they assert, would make the economic system flexible without running the risk of deflation and therefore large-scale unemployment and trade depression. Also, it would not be necessary to interfere with production in any direct fashion. It could be done by financial control, that is, by expanding and contracting credit facilities.

This is a solution highly attractive to certain types of mind that prefer ingenuity to the more painful process of deciding on first principles. If we descend from the lofty heights where abstractions reign and think in terms of concrete realities, what this device means is that decisions on what are to be production priorities are to be decided by bankers. Such a state of affairs would be wholly inconsistent with democracy. It would soon lead to trouble on a large scale.

In the absence of clear directives bankers have no way of deciding to whom to lend money except by the test of credit-worthiness. This means the possibility of a profit. The greater the prospect of a profit the more credit-worthy. So we are back where we started. But there are always prospects of profits on a rising market. Mere prospects of profit-making as the basis of lending would consequently lead directly to inflation. It would not be the substitution of one kind of consumption for another. It would mean an attempt to achieve all kinds of consumption simultaneously with no consideration of priority except the cash nexus. This has already been recognized in Britain where the banking houses have received directives from the Treasury to guide them in the issuing of credit. Armament is the test. When this is over the test will be full employment without inflation. That is to say, if promises are kept. So in neither case will it be possible to dodge the obligation of determining economic priorities. This is inescapable wherever some overriding principle is at work other than the rate of profit.

Controlled unemployment as a substitute for purposeful interference with the automatism of the price mechanism is consequently no substitute at all. As controls will be necessary in both cases, controlled plenty would seem to be more reasonable than controlled misery.

Of course, there is no exact comparison between the aim of full employment and the aim of arms production. In the latter case, what is intended is a certain type of production – arms. In the former, merely full production without regard to what is produced. One is quantitative, the other qualitative. But what we started to inquire into is just what is to give way in conditions of full employment if some forms of production are required as against others.

It was this situation that faced the British Labour government during the whole of its period of office. And the present Conservative administration has also to face it. If there is no economic slack to be taken up then preferences have to be made and much heart burning is the result. Thus Labour had to insist that homes for workers should take precedence over motion picture theatres, hotels and luxury building, and that industries producing for the export market, along with investment in basic industries that had been neglected when the profit motive alone counted, should become top priorities. There is no escape from the dilemma that if full employment is considered a social good, then qualitative selection among different claimants for credit facilities is inevitable.

It is here we begin to see what is behind the device of controlled unemployment. It is an effort to get away from the painful task of deciding what is the most desirable kind of consumption pattern to aim at. For those who swear by quantitative controls, pure and simple, a certain margin of unemployment is a desirable end. It may present another kind of picture to the unemployed themselves, but so long as they are not sufficiently numerous to be an electoral liability the political consequences of their protests can be ignored.

As I write, the London *Times* of 16 January 1952 reports an almost perfect example of the defence of an investment policy which relies exclusively on private initiative regardless of social objectives. It is contained in the speech of Anthony William Tuke, Chairman of Barclays, Limited, one of our four most important banks. The speech is a full-blooded attack on public planning and on state intervention in economic affairs. Among other matters, he criticizes the Labour government's housing policy. 'Personally,' he pontificates, 'I feel certain that the insistence of the Labour government on retaining this activity so largely in public hands has caused quite needless inflation of the price of these new houses. I believe that if private enterprise had been allowed to operate freely in this field subject only to control of design and construction and to a ceiling price, the result, given the co-operation of the trade unions concerned, would have been a lowering of the price of the finished article.' Later on, in the same speech, as though determined to plumb the depths of fatuity, he deplored the consequences for Great Britain of the shortage of coal. Now if the reader will consider those two statements together, he will begin to see how dangerous it is to allow the Tukes of this world to have their way. He laments the shortage of coal, which means of coal miners, which in its turn means more houses are needed in the mining districts. At the same time, he would allow private enterprise to build houses where it likes, for those willing to buy them on loans from building societies. This might begin to make sense if private enterprise would give preference to houses in the mining areas, and if the miners wanted to put themselves in debt to buy them. But that is precisely what did not and would not happen. The building of houses to rent was entrusted to the public authorities, because that was the only way of getting houses to those people whose services were most needed by the nation. Reliance upon the profit motive would have resulted in the building of houses for those whose work was less urgently required by the community. An additional proof of this is to be found in the fact that even the permitted quota of houses to be built for private ownership was not taken up in many of the mining districts.

The same story is true of the agricultural districts. Next to the need for more coal production is the urgent necessity to grow more food on our own land. It was possible to get the builders to build houses in the deep countryside only by denying them the right to build in the urban areas bordering on the agricultural belts. Here again the only agency available to build for the agricultural workers was the public authorities who could build for letting. The speculative builder is useless to the agricultural worker.

The distribution of labour in Britain is dangerously weighted against the industries we depend upon for our survival. These are in the main coal, steel, and agriculture. The policy advocated by people like Mr Tuke would starve them of homes and aggravate still further the ominous ill-balance of the labour force in Britain. It was a piece of good fortune for Britain that such troglodyte views were not let loose in the years immediately following the war. Mr Tuke, and those who think like him, must begin to learn that we could manage to survive without money-lenders and stockbrokers. We should find it harder to do without miners, steel workers and those who cultivate the land.

But it will be noted that even Mr Tuke is compelled to qualify his support for private enterprise. He would nobble it. So difficult is it to make the urge for profit conform to decent standards of behaviour that he would insist on conditions as to design, construction and price. These would entail form filling, licences, proscriptions, and supervision; all the paraphernalia of the planning he so deeply loathes.

One more word and I have finished with Mr Tuke. If the provision of houses during the difficult early postwar years had fed the greed of the money-lender and been conditioned by the size of the purse, we should not have enjoyed the immunity from civil strife that we did. The demobilized soldier would not have appreciated the finer points of Mr Tuke's economics. Even as it was we had a wave of forcible seizure of accommodation in 1946. It is easy to lecture, now that the dangerous period is past. We listen with scant patience to the homilies of Conservative bankers, for the positions they now abuse were rendered more secure by the rejection of their policies.

One way out of the dilemma of what to do without, when a sudden additional demand is made, as in the case of the arms programme, is to meet it by increased production. This is a much less painful process than cutting back civilian consumption. No pressure groups have to be resisted, no votes are endangered, and above all, no general education in the facts of our economic life is needed.

This was the goal set for itself by the American administration.
The people of the United States were to have both guns and butter.
Time, on 31 December 1951 reported under the heading 'The
Great Gamble':

> 'In 1951, said Defence Mobilizer Charles Wilson, we took a
> gamble . . . perhaps the greatest gamble in our history. By "we",
> Charlie Wilson meant the United States of America. The gamble
> was that U.S. business could expand fast enough to (1) pro-
> duce the arms needed for possible war, and (2) furnish the
> U.S. people with all – or almost all – the civilian goods they
> wanted.'

As *Time* went on to point out, the gamble did not quite come off.
Civilian goods, and even luxury goods, production was kept at a
phenomenally high level, but the arms targets were not reached.
Since then President Truman has warned that 1952, and possibly
1953, will see a cutback in civilian consumption. But the goal still
remains, that is, to meet the whole increased arms programme of the
United States by increased production capacity.

There is no reason to suppose that, given time, she will fail.
Already additional machines and plant have been provided equal
to almost seventy per cent of the national output of Britain. Steel
production is planned to reach 120 million tons a year, or more than
half the world production. This year the U.S.A. will devote to
arms 15 million tons more steel than the total steel output of the
Soviet Union. Equal and even greater results have been achieved
in other branches of industry.

American industrialists are justifiably proud of what they have
accomplished. And so they might be. Judged as a feat of technical
skill and energy it is breathtaking. It is a triumph of the mechanical
arts. Its other implications, for the strategy of diplomacy, I have
dealt with in the last chapter. Here I am concerned with the
consequences of this staggering spate of production for the
economic prospects of the world. Let us reflect a little on what all
this means.

What would happen if all of us applied the art of extracting and fabricating the raw materials of the earth with the same amount of success? Has anyone attempted to work out the consequences? Are we sure the raw materials are there? Especially the precious metals. Copper and zinc, for example? At the moment there is plenty of iron ore in sight, although even this is running ominously short in certain areas. We are nearing the exhaustion of tin. Of course, the optimists try to shout down our doubts by asserting the endless ingenuity of man in finding new sources of supply and in discovering substitutes. But would not elementary prudence counsel that we should have a look round and assess our resources before we run through them in this prodigal fashion?[37]

It must be kept in mind that the U.S.A. is not spending her own resources alone. She is spending the common stock of mankind. The U.S.A., as Governor Dewey pointed out a little time ago, imports more than ninety raw materials from outside her borders, all essential for her industries. Of course she is buying them with her dollars. In the language of commerce that ends the matter. But we may be reaching a situation where the commercial answer may not suffice.

One reason why the world shortage of raw materials slowed down the arms programme of the Western Powers is because the tempo of the fabricating industries is so much faster than that of the extracting industries; and also, of course, because the more immediately accessible metals have been exhausted and we are having to go farther afield for new supplies. It is easier to turn out the blueprints for a production line than it is to discover and then extract the precious metals with which to feed it.

This has caused some superficial observers to argue that the problem is therefore merely a technical one of timing the two processes so that the extracting industries are brought in line with the time schedules of the fabricating plants. Of course this is true on a short view – a very short view. But it also implies a nervous dependence on supplies from beyond a nation's own borders and therefore the temptation which appears as a necessity to interfere with the politics of the supplying nation. We have witnessed this in Persia, in Egypt, and in Malaya. Recently an E.C.A. project was launched to provide rail transport in Rhodesia for the purpose

of facilitating the extraction of precious metals. The agreement*
states: 'Such improvement of facilities will materially assist the
production and transport of certain materials produced within
Northern and Southern Rhodesia, such as cobalt, chrome, copper,
and tungsten, which are required by the Government of the United
States as the result of deficiencies in resources within the United
States.' A railway supplied on such terms is no longer a straight-
forward enterprise in international investment earning its dividends
by the profitability of the railway system alone. It is a tie-up of a
quite different kind, far removed from the simple transactions of a
free enterprise economy.

But the most serious immediate problem is that these raw
materials are physically exhaustible and when exhausted irreplace-
able. I repeat here the question I asked earlier. Suppose the rest of
the world, or even Europe alone, burned up scarce materials at
the same pace as the United States of America? Let me quote again
from *Time* (31 December 1951). It is a fascinating study of how
little insight can go along with a great deal of knowledge. Talking
of some of the difficulties the rearmament programme is encounter-
ing, the article goes on to say:

'In E.C.A.'s place Congress has authorized a maximum of six
billion dollars in the fiscal year 1952 for economic aid and to help
Europe rearm. But the rearmament effort has already wiped out
much of E.C.A.'s gain. In the last eighteen months, Europe's
prices shot up (France by thirty per cent), her currencies
weakened and the dollar gap widened at year's end to three
point-five billion dollars. This trouble arose because there was
so little slack in the European economies to take up the arms
load. Furthermore, despite all the missionary work of E.C.A.
and United States businessmen, European industries are woefully
inefficient by United States standards and still favour cartels
and monopolies rather than the United States brand of free

*'Agreement Between the Government of the United Kingdom of Great
Britain and Northern Ireland and the Government of the United States of
America. Relative to the Development of the Rhodesia Railways.'
(H.M.S.O., 6d. Cmd. 8396.)

enterprise. European businessmen blandly ignored the example of the United States in 1951; they, too, could expand their economies to bear the arms burden more easily, if they prized competitive freedom as highly as personal freedom. Without such a change, the vast new plants which the United States threw up in 1951 will make it harder than ever for European nations to compete in world markets or sell in the United States.'

Having said all this, the magazine then goes on to make a comment which makes nonsense of it all.

'*Apart from money*', it comments, '*the United States had to re-assess how far it could stretch its own natural resources. The vast new expansion was using up such minerals as iron, copper and lead far faster than anyone had anticipated only a few years ago. In many ways the United States, once the owner of seemingly inexhaustible natural treasure, was in danger of becoming a have-not nation.* The end of the fabulously rich ores of the Mesabi Range was already in sight. Steelmakers not only began shipping in ore from South America and Liberia, but in 1951 they began operating plants to make the poor-grade taconite ore usable. Copper became so scarce that some metal producers talked of a permanent copper shortage (and saw aluminium taking its place in many ways). *In 1951 the United States tried to fill its need for raw materials by grabbing them in the world market. But in 1952 the United States would have to do more sharing and tailor its domestic needs more closely to the needs of all the Western nations.*' (My italics.)

The absurdities contained in these quotations are not the fault of *Time*. If they were merely that, they would not be worth quoting and answering in a work of this nature. I call attention to them because they put the fundamental defects of the American way of life so clearly, if unconsciously.

Europe is reproached because she does not produce as efficiently as the United States. The United States will not be able to produce as much as she hoped this year because she will have to share scarce raw materials with Europe. So if Europe produced as efficiently as

the United States there would be an even greater quantity of idle
plant in both continents. Thus the greater the productive efficiency
the more plants would be idle. Nevertheless *Time* deplores the
failure of Europe to imitate the efficiency of America's production
methods. The spectacle therefore afforded us by the United States
is one of technical brilliance and social blindness. Given the present
state of knowledge, if the rest of the world was able to fabricate
materials with the facility of the United States, the plants could not
be operated. The free enterprise economies would have worked
themselves to a partial standstill. I do not say that this would
necessarily be a permanent condition. We may at some time be able
to run a mechanically based civilization without using metals and
minerals – at least those quickly exhausted. But we have not reached
that stage yet by any means. At the rate we are going we are sawing
off the limb on which we are sitting – and the defenders of the
acquisitive competitive system invite us to admire the sharpness of
the saw.

This expansionist process, pursued without regard to its ultimate
possibility of real value in terms of human happiness and good-will,
was enormously accelerated by two world wars and now by preparation for the third. For example, the United States increased its
steel production during the last war by more than the total British
output at the time. Nevertheless, war only emphasized the principles
which are innate in the competitive system, and these arise from a
chronic incapacity for discriminating selection and a just apportion-
ing of the national product. We are told by a spokesman of the
United States steel interests that the decision to expand further steel
production was taken before the Korean war.

The consequences of all this is to create such a state of ill-balance
between the dollar world and the rest, as to give rise to alarm
bordering on panic as to what will happen when the rearmament
drive is over – if, that is to say, we are fortunate enough to escape
war in the meantime. All the world, outside the Soviet-dominated
bloc, will be geared to the economy of the United States. We have
already learned what that means, even before the latest gigantic
rise in the United States productive capacity takes effect. A recession of only four per cent in employment in the United States was

sufficient to produce a crisis in Europe. A recent report published*
by the United Nations grimly underlines the danger. It points out
that if a similar recession follows rearmament, and it results in the
same order of disturbance, then the dollar income of the outside
world would be reduced in two years by 10,000 million dollars,
equal to a quarter of the total income. In 1947 these countries held
reserves totalling about fifty per cent of the annual value of their
imports. The proportion is now only twenty-five per cent. It would
not therefore need a major slump to finish those reserves within a
year. If nothing is done to deal with that situation Stalin will not
need to lift a finger. The capitalist system will do the job for him.

It is quite possible, indeed it is even probable, that there are
immense deposits of precious metals and minerals yet to be sur-
veyed and discovered that would add many more years of consumption for the mechanical arts. It is very much to be hoped that there
are. Otherwise the outlook is black for those nations that have
scarcely started to nibble at them. The attempt to discover them
should be undertaken at once. This should be done not by private
adventure but by some agency of the United Nations acting for
the whole world, so that they could be extracted under reasonable
conditions for the nations and peoples immediately concerned, and
shared among the consuming countries in accordance with some
carefully worked-out plan of priorities. Unless this is done we shall
reach crippling physical limits to what we can do to lift the standards
of material comfort for the backward peoples.

More and more stress needs to be laid on the use of machinery
for the cultivation of products of the surface soils. The absence of
a plan for putting first things first is creating a macabre situation.
Soon, if we are not more prudent, millions of people will be watching each other starve to death through expensive television sets. If
action at the governmental level had not been taken for the stimulation of agricultural production in Britain the standards of food
consumption of her people would be even lower than they are: so
hopelessly inadequate was competitive capitalism as an agency for
meeting the needs of the people.

*Measures for International Economic Stability. Obtainable at H.M.S.O.

G

It is newsprint, however, that provides the most striking illustration of the present anarchy in world production and consumption. The United States, with one-fifteenth of the world's population, consumed in 1950 well over two-thirds of the world newsprint supplies. It had increased its average pre-war per capita consumption by fifty per cent, while the United Kingdom suffered a decrease of more than fifty per cent. Nearly every European country, along with New Zealand and Australia, suffered a fall from pre-war consumption. Some idea of the impact of the American demand on world supplies can be gained from the fact that a one per cent cut in American consumption would enable Britain to abolish tonnage rationing and restricted circulation and go back to six page newspapers as a step to further increases. A reduction of twenty-five per cent in American consumption would still leave her more than nine per cent above pre-war and allow other countries to reach their pre-war consumption.[38]

It is true that many countries have large illiterate populations, but this is really beside the point, because even if they could all read, no more newsprint would be available for them.

Over the past year the price of paper has gone up 100 per cent. It is now between five and six times higher than pre-war. The consequences of all this for Britain are further aggravated by the concentration of newspaper ownership in fewer hands and by the huge circulations of the national dailies and weeklies. In one year alone – 1951 – fifty journals ceased publication. The same thing is happening in many other countries.

Faced with these facts, what is the use of talking of a 'free press'? If it is true, and I believe it is, that a free press is an essential condition for the functioning of a democracy, then these figures bear no other interpretation than that democracy is being strangled more effectively by the normal operations of the capitalist system than by the military threat of Soviet Communism. Without free expression of opinion and the means to ensure it a democracy dies. Its death is no less certain because it occurs stealthily and by the slow silting-up of the channels of communication. What is the use of demanding the extension of democratic self-government to countries where it does not now exist and then denying democracy the very breath of life by an unrestrained gobbling up of the world's supply of newsprint?

Of all monopolies, monopoly of opinion is the worst. Of all forms of consumption, aside from food itself, that of free and therefore diversified opinion should be the persistent aim of a civilized society. Yet it is the one form of consumption which has failed to regain prewar levels, apart from the United States, Canada, Sweden, Switzerland, and one or two countries where in any case the consumption was infinitesimal. A New York citizen will stagger along under the weight of a ninety-page Sunday newspaper, which he will never have either the time or the inclination to read through. In Great Britain it cannot be said that smaller supplies are put to better use. The newspaper owners are bullied by their swollen circulations. The smallest recession produces an 'office crisis'. The British people have never been less informed about what is happening in the rest of the world. A large proportion of the tiny space now left to the national dailies and weeklies is devoted to deliberate pornography or to retailing the minutest details of the lives of the royal family. Indeed, the latter has now reached a point where it has become a national disgrace. It must be deeply repugnant to the persons immediately concerned, who are carrying out difficult duties with commendable dignity and restraint.

A sort of newspaper Gresham's Law appears to be operating where only bad standards of journalism are commercially successful. The prevailing shortage of newsprint means that the career of journalism no longer offers adequate opportunities for high quality work. The small circulation magazines and local papers are not present in sufficient quantity to provide a means of recruitment for new talent and diverse effort. The resulting impoverishment is all the more deadly because it is insidious and hardly noticed. It is a state of affairs that must occasion anxiety to all who value the position of the newspaper in the life of the nation.

There is only one corrective for this and it is the one denied us: cheap and plentiful supplies of newsprint so that it is comparatively easy to start new journals and so seek out a readership now rendered inarticulate by the mass circulations. Neither the governments nor the private interests concerned can plead that they have stumbled blindly into this newsprint crisis without knowing what was happening to them. There is nothing new in the facts that I have here set out. They have been reported and commented upon in section every of the press. But so far private initiative has failed to find the remedy.

We cannot rely entirely on former sources of supply. We must search out substitute materials. An urgent effort should be made at once, before the present cultural decline degenerates into torpor.

NOTE 37

'The Sulphur Committee of the International Materials Conference this evening announced the allocation of crude sulphur for the first six months of this year. This is the first time any of the conference committees has adopted the longer period of six months for such allocation, and this change will, it is thought, prove to be of considerable help to countries making procurements. Out of a total of 2,953,400 long tons of crude sulphur the United States is allocated 2,226,000 tons and the United Kingdom 194,900.

'The committee pointed out that in preparing this plan of distribution it had been confronted with the fact that estimated requirements of sulphur for 1952 totalled 7,364,100 long tons, while estimated production was only 5,625,100 tons — leaving a gap of 1,739,000 tons.' – Washington Correspondent of *The Times*, 25 January, 1952.

NOTE 38

Consumption of Newsprint per Head of Population in Certain
Countries in 1950 and 1951

The following data are taken from two reports on *World Communications*, published by the United Nations Educational, Scientific and Cultural Organization, as specified:

(1) *World Communications: Press, Radio, Film,* May 1950 (UNESCO publication, No. 700), pp. 164–173.

(2) *World Communications: Press, Radio, Film, Television,* July 1951 (UNESCO publication, No. 942), pp. 166–175.

Area and Country	Consumption of newsprint per inhabitant in kilograms (a) in 1950 report	(b) in 1951 report
AFRICA		
Egypt	1.00	0.70
Union of South Africa	4.20	5.00
NORTH AMERICA		
Canada*	21.10	22.50
U.S.A.	32.50	33.60
ASIA		
Burma	0.80	0.10
China	0.10	n.a.
India	0.10	0.10
Iraq	0.07	0.20
Israel	4.20	3.60
Jordan	n.a.	0.20
Lebanon	0.90	0.80
Pakistan	0.06	0.06
Persia	0.06	0.09
Saudi Arabia	n.a.	0.02
Syria	n.a.	0.20
Thailand (Siam)	0.10	0.10
Turkey	0.47	0.50
United States of Indonesia	0.05	0.05
EUROPE		
Belgium	7.60	7.50
France	5.20	6.60
Ireland (Eire)	6.00	7.00
Italy	1.50	1.60
Netherlands	5.90	5.80
Norway	7.60	7.40
Spain	0.80	0.80
Sweden	15.80	15.70
Switzerland	11.00	10.80

n.a. = not available.
* Including Newfoundland and Labrador.

Area and Country	Consumption of newsprint per inhabitant in kilograms	
	(a) *in 1950* report	(b) *in 1951* report
U.S.S.R.*	1.70	1.70
United Kingdom	8.30	13.80
OCEANIA		
Australia	11.80	16.00
New Zealand	12.80	14.00

*Including Byelorussia and Ukraine.

10

Democratic Socialism

'AFTER the first death, there is no other.' With that lovely and tender line the poet Dylan Thomas ends a poem on the death of a child killed in a fire-raid on London. The poet here asserts the uniqueness of the individual personality. If the imagination can plumb the depths of a personal tragedy, no multiplication of similar incidents can add to the revelation. Numbers can increase the social consequences of disaster, but the frontiers of understanding are reached when our spirit fully identifies itself with the awful loneliness and finality of personal grief.

The capacity for emotional concern for individual life is the most significant quality of a civilized human being. It is not achieved when limited to people of a certain colour, race, religion, nation or class. Indeed, just to the extent that this or that group commands our exclusive sympathy, we are capable of the most monstrous cruelty, or at best indifference, to others who do not belong to the group. Describing a hanging scene at Tyburn gaol not so much more than a hundred years ago, the learned and observant diarist, Charles Greville, 'was astonished by the incomprehensible attitude of some of the boys sentenced to be hanged. Never,' he is reported as saying, 'did I see boys cry so.'*

These children belonged to a different social class from Greville's. Their terror apparently made no claim on his emotions or understanding. In much the same way the Nazis put the Jews outside the walls of their personalities, except as objects of sadistic pleasure. So, too, races of a different colour from their own, or groups that stand in the way of their ambitions, are regarded by some of our contemporaries.

*_The London Anthology_, by Pauline and Hugh Massingham (Macmillan, 1951, p. xii).

Not even the apparently enlightened principle of the 'greatest good for the greatest number' can excuse indifference to individual suffering. There is no test for progress other than its impact on the individual. If the policies of statesmen, the enactments of legislatures, the impulses of group activity, do not have for their object the enlargement and cultivation of the individual life, they do not deserve to be called civilized.

It is its preoccupation with the needs of the individual that has caused Democratic Socialism to be called 'dull'. Some visitors to Britain during the lifetime of the 1945 Labour government commented on what they described as the 'universal greyness of the social climate'. And, of course, on the scarcity of porterhouse steaks in the fashionable restaurants. Rationing and 'fair shares' in the necessities of life were so 'dull'. They complained of the 'lack of colour' in the cities. If they had looked closer they would have seen the roses in the cheeks of the children and the pride and self-confidence of the young mothers. They would have found that more was being done for working people than in any other part of the world at that time.

Where wealth is concentrated in few hands the outcome is ostentatious spending and the meretricious glamour that goes with it. The accompanying social climate lends a certain superficial circumstantiality to the claim that only the competitive society is pervaded by a spirit of 'adventure'. It is more 'adventurous' to have a number of millionaires than it is to spend the money wasted by them on curing and preventing ill-health. The fashionable magazines and newspapers neon-light the petty foibles of the well-to-do. Through the dazzle it is not easy to see the mass of discomfort and downright misery which is the other side of the picture.

The attempt of Democratic Socialism to universalize the consumption of the best that society can afford meets with resistance from those whose sense of values is deformed by the daily parade of functionless wealth. When wealth is dispersed and distributed in scores of millions of homes the result is not so conspicuous. The social scene provides fewer dramatic contrasts. But there is no doubt about which type of society produces more quiet contentment and political stability.[39]

When the ordinary man and woman is disfranchised, as in the dictatorship countries, the emphasis on the public spectacle is still greater. Consumption by pageantry takes the place of private consumption. Vicarious consumption has a subtle and dangerous influence on human psychology. If your own life is one of poverty and powerlessness, there is a tendency to seek compensation in institutions with which it is easy for you emotionally to identify yourself. This probably explains why the poorest members of the community are often the most chauvinistic. The well-known bellicosity of dictatorships is therefore fed by a morbid desire for the enjoyment of vicarious power by the politically helpless masses. It is not only that coercion and bullying come easily to those who have climbed to power by these means and who maintain themselves there by similar methods: it is also because the whole social psychology of such communities is perverted by the horrible contrast between individual weakness on the one hand and the pomp of unbridled power on the other.

It is therefore no accident that it is among the solid artisan classes that you will find the most tolerance and the least belligerency. Their attitude corresponds most closely with that of Democratic Socialism. Their lives are rounded by the consciousness of acquired skills and by the rhythm of daily labour which lead to a wholesome psychology needing no compensation in flag-waving and drum-beating. They have little taste for the 'grandest adventure of all' – war.

The philosophy of Democratic Socialism is essentially cool in temper. It sees society in its context with nature and is conscious of the limitations imposed by physical conditions. It sees the individual in his context with society and is therefore compassionate and tolerant. Because it knows that all political action must be a choice between a number of possible alternatives it eschews all absolute proscriptions and final decisions. Consequently it is not able to offer the thrill of the complete abandonment of private judgement, which is the allure of modern Soviet Communism and of Fascism, its running mate. Nor can it escape the burden of social choice so attractively suggested by those who believe in *laissez-faire* principles and in the automatism of the price system. It accepts the obligation to choose among different kinds of social action and in so doing to bear the pains of rejecting what is not practicable or less desirable.

Democratic Socialism is a child of modern society and so of relativist philosophy. It seeks the truth in any given situation, knowing all the time that if this be pushed too far it falls into error. It struggles against the evils that flow from private property, yet realizes that all forms of private property are not necessarily evil. Its chief enemy is vacillation, for it must achieve passion in action in the pursuit of qualified judgements. It must know how to enjoy the struggle, while recognizing that progress is not the elimination of struggle but rather a change in its terms.

In the beginning of this book I discuss political power and how the problem of attaining it appeared to young workers like myself in the industrial towns and cities of Britain. We were pre-occupied with how to raise the general standard of life. The pursuit of power presented itself to us in social and not in personal terms. It is clearer to me now than it was then that the nation is too small an arena in which to hope to bring the struggle to a final conclusion. This is true whether the nation is large or small. Thus the attainment of political power in the modern state still leaves many problems outside its scope. National sovereignty is a phrase which history is emptying of meaning.

Many seeing this are inclined to turn away from the difficult task of establishing Socialism in their own country. They say, 'What is the use of doing so? We shall still find ourselves possessed of only a partial victory. Only world victory will suffice, so let us concentrate on that.' This is an engaging and seductive view and many have succumbed to it. *We are all acquainted with the world statesman who is for ever making global constitutions while the one nearest him is in the control of someone else. If you are going to plan the world you must first of all control the part of it that you will want to fit into the whole.* International organizations are continually passing the most idealistic resolutions that remain in the air because the statesmen subscribing to them are without the economic power to carry them out. The assumption behind these activities is that social and economic conditions derive from political constitutions. But the reverse is the case. An old teacher used to tell me, concerning nations and constitutions, 'The man's clothes are there because the man is there; not the man there because the man's clothes are there. A nation is a nation before it gets a constitution.' The constitution is the codification of an accomplished fact.

This is not an argument against international co-operation. On the contrary, one of the main themes of this book is a plea for more and more international co-operation. But this would be given greater reality in action, if the governments of the world could speak with authority for the economic behaviour of their own peoples.

Looking back over more than thirty-five years of industrial and political activity I find no reason to alter my conviction that the principles of Democratic Socialism are the only ones broadly applicable to the situation in which mankind now finds itself.

NOTE 39

Visiting Italy in 1948, I saw cinemas in course of construction for which imported steel was being used. In Britain we had forbidden the use of structural steel even in house-building, as we needed all we had for the building of factories, power stations and engineering exports. While Italian cinemas were consuming precious steel, and skilled labour, there were villages and towns that had been razed to the ground during the war where not one brick had been laid on another. It was clear that the consequence of this and of other failures to attend to the needs of the common people as against the greed of a few would result in the growth of the Communist Party even in the traditionally Conservative South. I said so to members of the Italian government at the time. And so it proved.